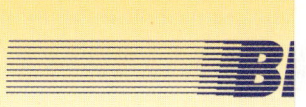

# Pediatric Emergencies
## *The First Five Minutes*

Grant B. Goold, MPA, EdD, EMT-P
Paul F. Marmen, MEd, BS, EMT

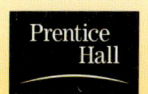

Prentice Hall
Upper Saddle River, New Jersey 07458

**Library of Congress Cataloging-in-Publication Data**
Goold, Grant B.
  The first five minutes: an injury prevention and pediatric emergency care handbook / Grant B. Goold, Paul F. Marmen.
    p.;cm.
  Includes index.
  ISBN 0-13-014573-4 (pbk.)
    1. Pediatric emergencies—Handbooks, manuals, etc.
  2. Children—Wounds and injuries—Prevention—Handbooks, manuals, etc.  3. First aid in illness and injury—Handbooks, manuals, etc.  I. Marmen, Paul F.  II. Title.
    [DNLM: 1. Emergency Treatment—methods—Child.
  2. Child Day Care Centers—organization & administration.
  3. Emergencies—Child.  4. Risk Management—methods.
  5. Wounds and Injuries—prevention & control—Child.
  WS 205 G659f2002]
  RJ370.G66 2002
  618.92'0025–dc21
                                        2002016988

**Publisher:** Julie Levin Alexander
**Executive Assistant:** Regina Bruno
**Senior Acquisitions Editor:** Katrin Beacom
**Editorial Assistant:** Kierra Kashickey
**Senior Marketing Manager:** Tiffany Price
**Product Information Manager:** Rachele Triano
**Director of Production and Manufacturing:** Bruce Johnson
**Managing Production Editor:** Patrick Walsh
**Manufacturing Manager:** Ilene Sanford
**Manufacturing Buyer :** Pat Brown
**Production Editor:** April Lippert, Navta Associates, Inc.
**Development/Copy Editor:** Terse Stamos
**Creative Director:** Cheryl Asherman
**Design Coordinator:** Maria Guglielmo-Walsh
**Cover Designer:** Blair Brown
**Composition:** Navta Associates, Inc.
**Printing and Binding:** The Banta Company

Pearson Education LTD.
Pearson Education Australia PTY, Limited
Pearson Education Singapore, Pte. Ltd
Pearson Education North Asia Ltd
Pearson Education Canada, Ltd
Pearson Educación de Mexico, S.A. de C.V.
Pearson Education—Japan
Pearson Education Malaysia, Pte. Ltd
Pearson Education, Upper Saddle River, New Jersey

**NOTICE ON CARE PROCEDURES**

The author and the publisher of this book have taken care to make certain that the equipment and schedules of treatment are correct and compatible with the standards generally accepted at the time of publication. Nevertheless, as new information becomes available, changes in treatment and in the use of equipment and procedures becomes necessary. The reader is advised to carefully consult the instruction and information material included in the piece of equipment or device before administration. First aid responders are warned that the use of any techniques must be authorized by their medical adviser, where appropriate, in accord with local laws and regulations. The publisher disclaims any liability, loss, injury, or damage incurred as a consequence, directly or indirectly, of the use and application of any of the contents of this book.

**NOTICE ON GENDER USAGE**

The English language has historically given preference to the male gender. Among many words, the pronouns "he" and "his" are commonly used to describe both genders. Society evolves faster than language, and the male pronouns still predominate in our speech. The authors have made great effort to treat the two genders equally, recognizing that a significant percentage of daycare personnel are female. However, in some instances, male pronouns may be used to describe both males and females solely for the purpose of brevity. This is not intended to offend any readers of the female gender.

---

Copyright © 2003 by Pearson Education, Upper Saddle River, New Jersey 07458. All rights reserved. Printed in the United States of America. This publication is protected by Copyright and permission should be obtained from the publisher prior to any prohibited reproduction, storage in a retrieval system, or transmission in any form or by any means, electronic, mechanical, photocopying, recording, or likewise. For information regarding permission(s), write to: Rights and Permissions Department.

**Prentice Hall**

10 9 8 7 6 5 4 3 2 1
ISBN 0-13-014573-4

## DEDICATION

To my wife Shelley, who has taught me the value of each and every child. To Kyla, Aubrey, Hunter, McKenna, and Haley for providing me ample opportunities to practice my pediatric assessments. Most importantly, to all those people willing to shape, mold, and love the future of our society. Keep up the good work!

G.B.G.

To my wife Rosemary, for her encouragement, love, and support. Also, to my grandchildren Jacob, Joshua, and Molly Rose for all the new things they keep teaching me about children. To the childcare professionals across this country that do a tremendous job providing a safe and healthy environment for our children.

P.F.M.

# CONTENTS

| | | |
|---|---|---|
| **Introduction** | | vii |

| SECTION 1 | **PREPAREDNESS** | |
|---|---|---|
| Chapter 1 | Prevention, Prevention, Prevention | 2 |
| Chapter 2 | PediScan Checklist | 13 |
| Chapter 3 | Disaster Planning | 20 |

| SECTION 2 | **UNIVERSAL SYMBOL TRAINING** | |
|---|---|---|
| Chapter 4 | Scene Safety | 26 |
| Chapter 5 | Standard Precautions | 29 |
| Chapter 6 | Initial Assessment | 32 |
| Chapter 7 | Ongoing Assessment | 36 |
| Chapter 8 | Activation of the Emergency Medical Services (EMS) System | 40 |
| Chapter 9 | Basic Life Support: Rescue Breathing (Artificial Ventilation) | 42 |
| Chapter 10 | Basic Life Support: Cardiopulmonary Resuscitation | 49 |
| Chapter 11 | Shock | 55 |
| Chapter 12 | Soft-Tissue Injury | 58 |
| Chapter 13 | Musculoskeletal Injury/Immobilization | 65 |
| Chapter 14 | Spinal Precautions | 69 |
| Chapter 15 | Oxygen Application | 72 |

| SECTION 3 | **INJURY AND ILLNESS TREATMENT** | |
|---|---|---|
| **Injury and Illness Quick Reference Guide** | | 76 |
| **Answers to Real-Life Response Treatment Questions** | | 105 |
| **Index** | | 109 |

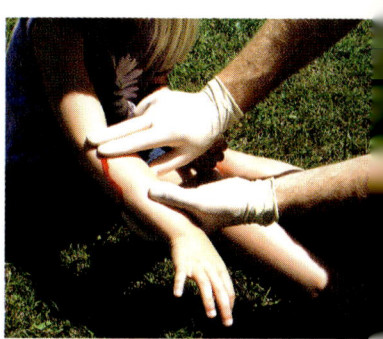

## ABOUT THE AUTHORS

**Grant B. Goold** is Program Director of the EMS Education Center at American River College in Sacramento. Grant holds a Master's Degrees in Public Administration and Health Services Administration. He holds a Doctorate in Education with special emphasis on educational technology from the University of San Francisco.

Grant serves on the Board of Directors for Sacramento Metropolitan Fire District. Grant provides training consultation to several childcare corporations and is currently developing training programs for the amusement park industry. He has authored several books on personal leadership, workplace safety, and prehospital first aid. Grant encourages comments on how to improve this pediatric first aid manual.

**Paul F. Marmen** is the director of the Emergency Medical Services for Children (EMSC) Resource Center at the University of Oklahoma Health Sciences Center. He is also the Manager of the Section of General Pediatrics, Pediatric Emergency Services, Department of Pediatrics at Children's Hospital, Oklahoma University Medical Center.

Paul holds a Master's degree in Professional Health Occupations Education and is the co-author of the Injury Prevention and First Care program for pediatric first aid used to educate childcare providers in Oklahoma. He is a member of the Oklahoma Healthy Child advisory council and currently serves in an advisory capacity on several state level committees and training programs for emergency medical services advocating improved pediatric emergency care and education. He has a 30-year career in health care, the last 18 years in EMS, and continues to work part-time as an EMT.

## REVIEWERS

**Brenda Beasley, RN, BS, EMT-Paramedic**
Department Chair, Allied Health
Calhoun College
Decatur, AL

**James C. Enos, NREMT-P**
Sarasota County Fire Department
Sarasota, FL

**Karen M. Joslin, EMT-I, BCLS-I**
Owner/Instructor, Heartbeats and Band-Aids
Des Moines, IA

**Ken Krupich, NREMT-P**
Paramedic Program Director
Fargo-Moorhead Ambulance Service
Fargo, ND

**David LaCovey, EMT-P**
EMS Coordinator
Children's Hospital of Pittsburgh
Pittsburgh, PA

**Daniel Limmer, EMT-P**
Faculty Member
Health Services Program
George Washington University
Washington, DC

**Wade W. Mitzel, NREMT-P**
BLS Coordinator/Instructor
Fargo-Moorhead Ambulance Service
Fargo, ND

**Nancy Thomas**
CDA Representative
Volunteer, Olympia Association
for the Education of Young Children
Library
Olympia, WA

**Dr. Phil Wishon**
Coordinator of Early Childhood
University of Northern Colorado
Greely, CO

# INTRODUCTION

We believe strongly in the famous saying, "A picture paints a thousand words." Research on adult learning has proven that adults retain information longer and understand ideas better when text is accompanied by visual cues. These cues can be in the form of simple pictures or icons. A symbol provides a very powerful cognitive link that is necessary during recall. In this handbook we call these visual cues, or icons, universal symbols. We are confident you will quickly learn the exact behavior and information represented by each symbol. Think of how quickly you comprehend a stop sign, wheelchair placard, traffic sign, or no smoking symbol.

*Everyday visual clues and symbols.*

Personal computer screens perhaps offer the best example of the use of icons or symbols to represent simple actions or complex tasks. Instead of using text or words to describe an action, a simple symbol or visual image is provided. You quickly learn that clicking on the printer symbol will trigger a certain action. The same learning processes that work for computer learners can work for childcare providers who wish to learn basic pediatric first aid and emergency care.

In more traditional pediatric first aid and emergency care training, a tremendous amount of time is spent reading or listening to detailed explanations of facts, figures, and procedures. Classes are generally text and

# INTRODUCTION

lecture-based. Students often complain about the lack of hands-on practice time. They also complain about the amount of material they forget once class is over. These concerns are supported by recent studies suggesting people attending traditional first aid and CPR training programs forget about 90 percent of what they learned in just a few short weeks after taking the class. To improve this situation, we developed this handbook and the universal symbols system.

It has been our experience that most students come to first aid classes to learn only what to do in the first few minutes. They come to learn only the basics and want a quick-and-easy method of recalling necessary emergency care steps. Childcare providers come to first aid and CPR classes to practice applying hands-on first aid skills. They want to feel that when the time comes to use those skills, they will be confident and able to act decisively.

The ultimate goal of this handbook is to give you life-saving, hands-on skills that you can quickly use and remember when seconds count. We emphasize the "need to know" skills and material and de-emphasize the "nice-to-know" information. Only very basic pediatric first aid information is included. By using the universal symbols system, we are able to eliminate most of the confusing and detailed written explanations. Most of the first aid skills are explained using actual photographs or drawings that demonstrate

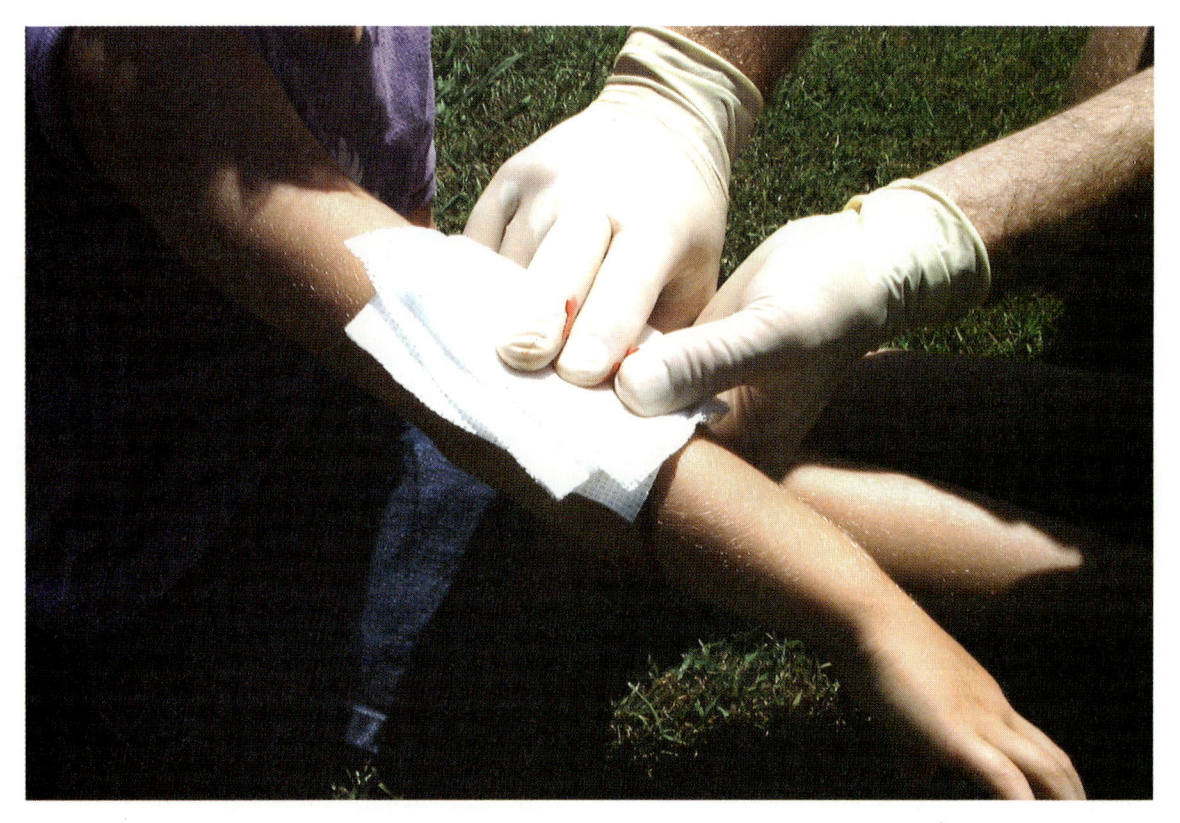

*Hands-on first aid skills for stopping bleeding.*

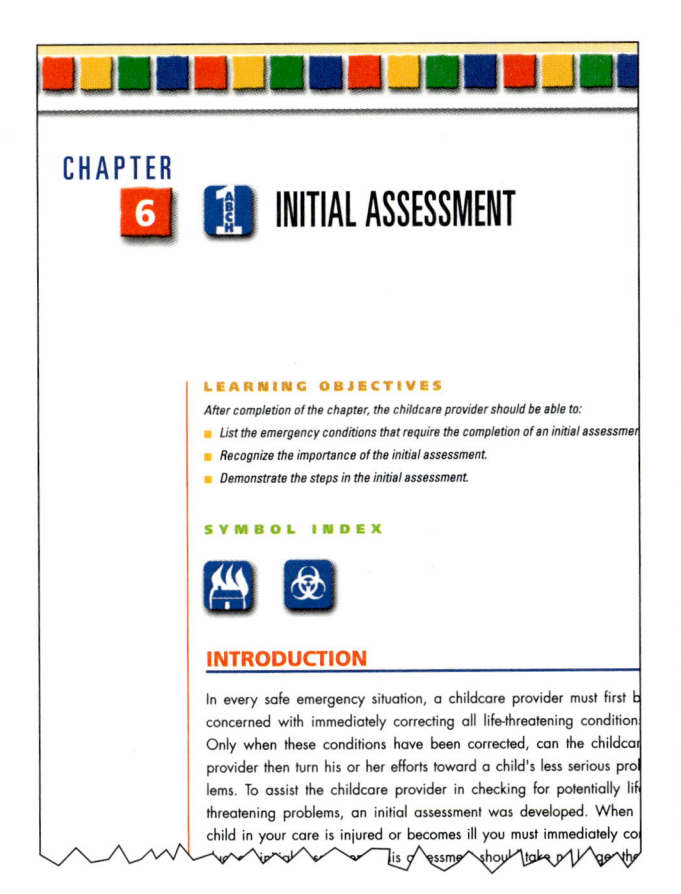

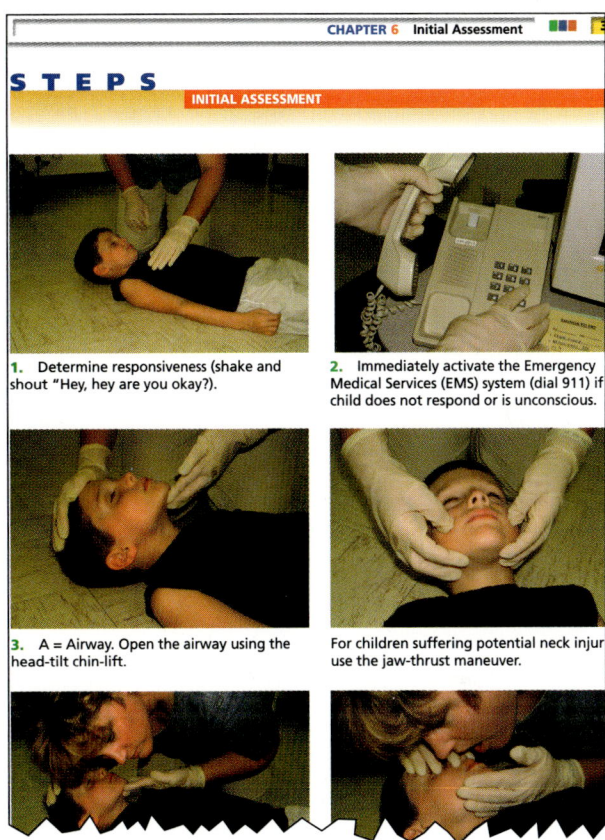

specific steps. These skills are then associated with a particular universal symbol. This symbol-skill association helps to simplify management of many pediatric emergency situations.

Each universal symbol represents some of the most common medical procedures and hands-on skills used in out-of-hospital emergency care. Mastery of the skills associated with each of the universal symbols provides you with the important information and simple action plans necessary to treat a majority of common pediatric emergencies.

As you progress through your training you will first gain a complete understanding of the skills associated with these universal symbols. Once you are comfortable with how each skill is performed and have had ample time to practice, you can then apply your knowledge of and skills related to each symbol to a long list of specific pediatric emergencies. You will quickly realize just how basic emergency first aid can be.

Each universal symbol is discussed in a separate chapter. Each chapter includes learning objectives, a brief introduction, a symbol index, treatment steps, danger signals, and a real-life response scenario. Answers to each real-life response are provided at the end of this handbook. Chapters 4–15 each include a symbol index. The symbol index for any given chapter may include previously learned symbols because they are also part of the general treatment addressed within that chapter.

# INTRODUCTION

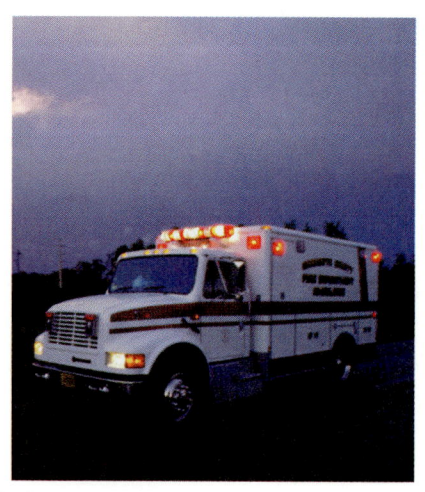

*Components of the EMS system include Emergency Medical Technicians, ambulance, and hospital.*

Basic pediatric emergency care offered in the first few minutes of an emergency is the most critical care a child will receive. By performing these life-saving skills, you offer drastically improved chances for the child's survival and enter the child into the Emergency Medical Services (EMS) system.

## Legal Protection

Many states have passed Good Samaritan laws that offer legal protection to those who render pediatric emergency care. These laws are designed to protect you. In order to prove negligence and liability, the court must find that you acted with malice, caused additional injury to the patient, did not act as a "reasonable person," and had a duty to render care. Good care is your best defense against lawsuits. Consult your local or state licensing agency to determine the exact nature of your duty to provide first aid care. Regardless of your duty to act and your experience with managing sick or injured children, if a child is pulseless and not breathing, he or she is clinically dead. In such situations, any proper care you render as a childcare provider will ultimately help improve the child's chances of survival.

## Using This Handbook

This handbook is separated into three sections. Section 1 provides introductory material regarding injury prevention, helpful checklists to improve the safety of your home or center, and information related to disaster planning. Section 2 includes content related to each of the universal symbols. Each chapter in this section capitalizes on your mastery of skills from the previous chapters. A symbol index is provided in several of the chapters to refresh your memory on the skills necessary to complete the tasks. Section 3 offers a quick reference guide to the care steps for the most common childhood emergencies encountered in childcare situations.

For maximum effect and long-term skills retention, we suggest that you review the symbol index at the beginning of each chapter in Section 2. If necessary, return to any specific universal symbol chapter to refresh your memory on the skills represented by the symbol.

## SYMBOL INDEX

## Keys to Training Success

We strongly encourage that each childcare provider practice the skills presented in this handbook using realistic workplace scenarios that involve injury patterns experienced in the past. We also suggest that every effort be made to frequently and regularly practice all of the skills represented by the universal symbols.

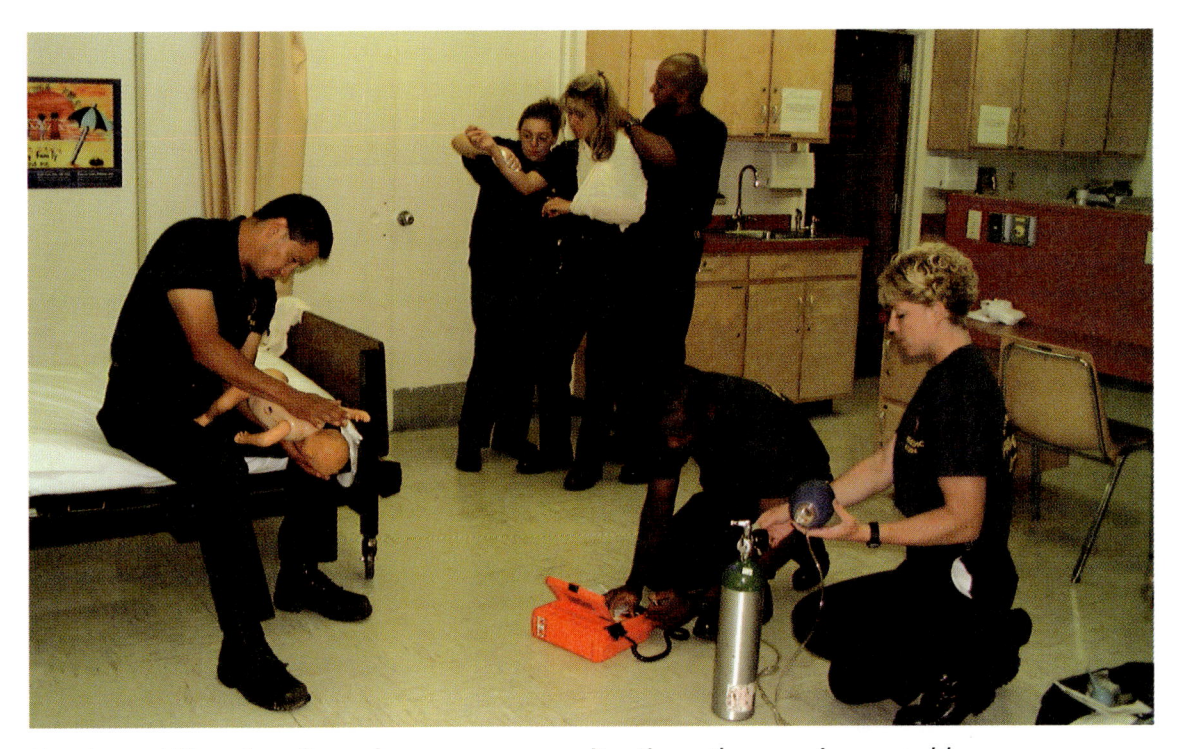

*Hands-on skill session. (In real emergency care situations, the caregivers would be wearing protective gloves.)*

## Stressing Prevention

No handbook on first aid and emergency care would be complete without some information on injury prevention. Each year between 20 to 25 percent of all children sustain injuries severe enough to require medical attention, missed school time, or bed rest. According to the National Center for Injury Prevention and Control:

- A child is injured in a playground every 2½ minutes.

- Children under the age of one account for almost 40 percent of mechanical suffocation and asphyxiation by foreign bodies.

- Pedestrian versus motor-vehicle collisions are the most common cause of serious head trauma for children between the ages of 5 and 9.

- Forty percent of all fatal bicycle deaths involve children ages 5–14.

- Burns are the fourth leading cause of unintentional injury death in the United States.

As the above statistics demonstrate, injuries can and do occur. Many pediatric injuries are the direct consequence of lack of supervision, unsafe environment, or careless behavior. Others result when someone cuts corners on safety in an effort to save time or money. Childcare providers must recognize the importance of providing and maintaining a safe and healthy environment. Basic injury prevention strategies and checklists are presented in Chapters 1 and 2.

Many organizations have injury prevention programs already in place. Find out what you can do to become actively involved in preventing and reducing injury. The more emphasis you place on prevention, the less likely you are to need your first aid and emergency care skills. One primary responsibility of all childcare providers is to emphasize prevention as often as possible.

## Remember the Basics

When faced with uncertainty most of us fall back into known behavior and comfort zones. The same is true in most emergency situations. Emergency situations can be so stressful that we can forget our training. If this happens, it is best for the injured child if we focus on basic skills, rather than completing more advanced care. Throughout this handbook we focus on the basics by repeatedly emphasizing the need to open the patient's airway, monitor breathing, and check circulation. It's that basic, as easy as A, B, C.

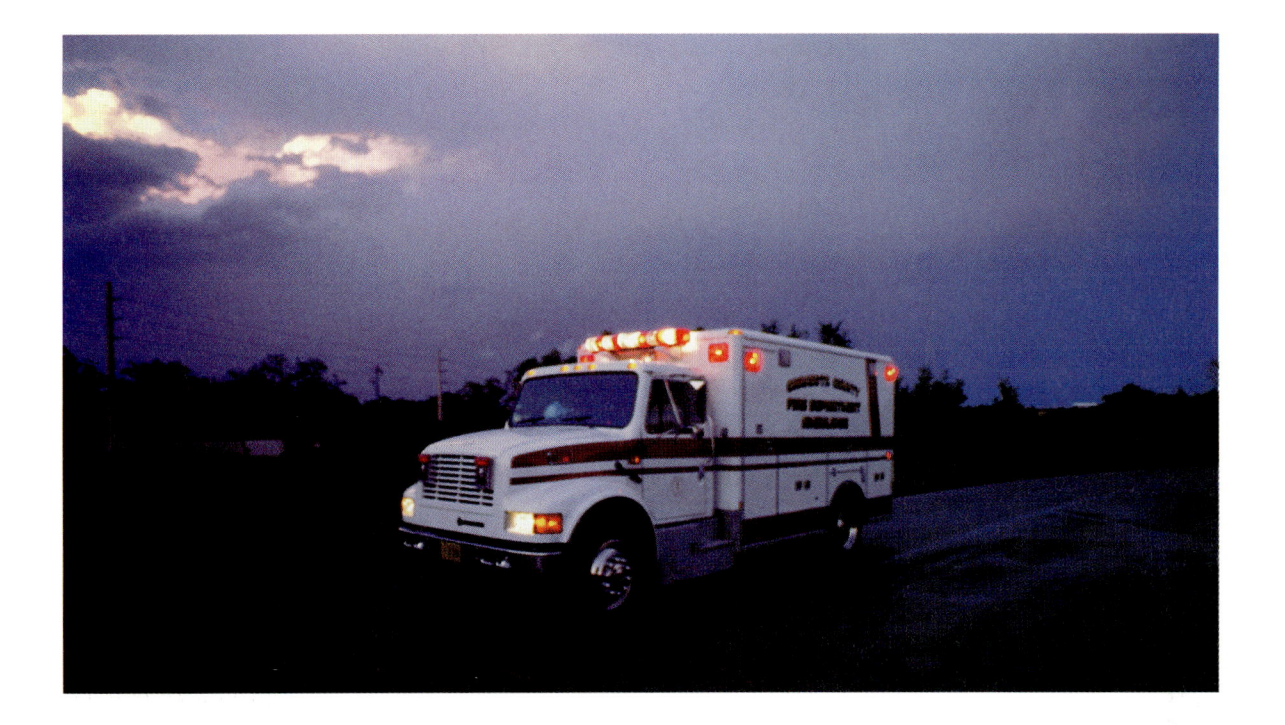

## Confidence

Confidence is the real key to performing successfully in many emergency situations. Mastery of the universal symbols and practicing their application under various conditions will help build your confidence. As a childcare team member you should determine which pediatric emergencies are most likely to occur in your setting and then practice the skills necessary to manage those emergencies. You can do it!

Enjoy this handbook, write in it, bend the pages, and share the information with others. Remember that the skills you are about to learn might one day save the life of a child, a friend, a family member, or your own.

# SECTION 1

# PREPAREDNESS

| | | |
|---|---|---|
| **Chapter 1** | Prevention, Prevention, Prevention | 2 |
| **Chapter 2** | PediScan Checklist | 13 |
| **Chapter 3** | Disaster Planning | 20 |

# CHAPTER 1

# PREVENTION, PREVENTION, PREVENTION

*"An ounce of prevention is worth a pound of cure."*
—Henry de Bracton

## INTRODUCTION

We have all heard this famous quote by Henry de Bracton. Yet how many childcare providers, including parents, realize that with a little planning and some diligence they can significantly reduce the chances of children being injured. Research continues to prove that prevention programs play the single most important role in reducing childhood injuries.

For the most part, children cannot understand when they are in a dangerous situation. They are naturally curious and willing to try everything and explore everywhere. So, the responsibility falls back to the caregiver to provide a safe environment. Ironically, the "ounce" of effort one invests to prevent injury often pays off with more than just one pound of cure; it pays off ten pounds, twenty pounds, or however much a child weighs. Not a bad return on your investment.

### Injury Prevention—Evidence of a Problem

Childhood injuries are relatively uncommon in childcare settings. However, training and education related to injury prevention and emergency first aid for infants and children are as important as are understanding the children's developmental stages, nutritional needs, program activities, infectious diseases, and other topics studied by the childcare provider. It is estimated that each year 240–320 children in childcare lose their lives. However, many states do not collect data on childcare injuries or deaths. Examples of injuries that have been reported include eye injuries from glass, a 13-month-old whose thumb was severed; a 10-month-old left in a bathtub with water running; a child hit by a car after getting out a center door; and a 3-month-old who suffocated in a crib with a diaper bag found over his face. All of these injuries could have been prevented.

## Emergency Medical Services Response Times

The average response time for most urban emergency medical services (EMS) is eight minutes. Eight minutes is a very long time during an emergency situation. Sit quietly for eight minutes and you will think you were sitting for twenty minutes. You are fortunate if your center or home is in an urban area where the response time is three to six minutes. However, if your center is in a rural community, response time could be twenty minutes or longer. In case of an injury to a child, remember you are the "on-the-scene" person. Your quick actions are critical to a child's health and welfare.

## Injury Reporting

When an injury occurs in a childcare center or in family home care, an Incident Report Form should be initiated (see page 5). Documentation of an injury is necessary for a number of reasons. However, your first consideration is giving appropriate first aid, and, if necessary, activating the EMS System. The Incident Report Form should be completed as soon after the injury as possible. Delay in completing the report may cause you to forget vital information regarding the cause, the care provided, or the essential follow-up which was not completed. Another

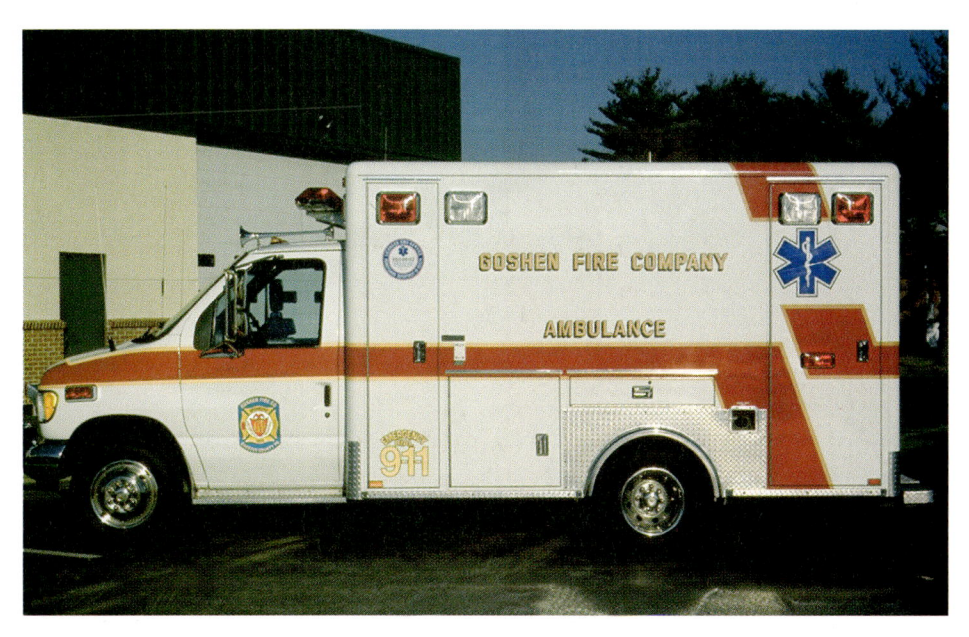

*The average response time for an EMS ambulance in an urban area is eight minutes.*

reason for completing the report is to assist the center staff in recognizing injury trends. Such documentation could provide background data needed to eliminate certain hazardous toys, playground equipment, activities, or furniture. Such data could also help you to modify your notification procedures. A final review by center staff of the Incident Report after follow-up care (if required) could provide the impetus for changes to policy or procedures.

The publication "Caring for Our Children: National Health and Safety Performance Standards for Out-of-Home Child Care" can provide you with additional information regarding the reporting of injuries that take place in childcare settings. It is available from the American Academy of Pediatrics bookstore at www.aap.org.

## Injury Prevention Strategies

Caring for children is a challenge. On one hand, you must ensure their safety; but on the other hand, you must allow them to grow and develop. It's often difficult to maintain just the right balance. The following five-point injury prevention plan should help you provide a safe middle ground in which children can flourish.

1. *Never underestimate what a child can do.* A newborn infant cannot fall off a bed, right? Wrong. A child cannot open a child-resistant container, right? Wrong again! Children learn fast, so play it safe and assume that children are more mobile and more dexterous than you ever thought possible.

2. *Teach safety.* Your goal is to help children learn how to be safe. If you explain safety precautions and consistently reinforce safe behavior, such as wearing helmets, eventually children will be able to make sound decisions about their well-being.

*Teaching proper safety behavior.*

# Incident Report Form

*Fill in all blanks and boxes that apply.*

Name of
Program:_____ Phone:_____
Address of Facility:_____

Child's Name:_____ Sex: M F Birthdate:___/___/___/IncidentDate:___/___/___/

Time of Incident: _____ am / pm Witnesses:

Name of Legal Guardian / Parent Notified:_____ Notified by:_____ TimeNotified:____:____ am / pm

EMS (911) or other medical professional Not notified Notified Time Notified:____:____ am / pm

Location where incident occurred: ☐ playground ☐ classroom ☐ bathroom ☐ hall ☐ kitchen ☐ doorway
☐ gym ☐ office ☐ dining room ☐ stairway ☐ unknown ☐ other (specify)_____

Equipment/product involved: ☐ climber ☐ slide ☐ swing ☐ playground surface ☐ sandbox ☐ trike/bike
☐ hand toy (specify):_____

Other equipment (specify):_____
Cause of injury: (describe)_____
☐ fall to surface; estimated height of fall ____ feet; type of surface:_____
☐ fall from running or tripping ☐ bitten by child ☐ motor vehicle ☐ hit or pushed ☐ by child ☐ injured by object
☐ eating or choking ☐ insect sting/bite ☐ animal bite ☐ injury from exposure to cold other(specify):_____

Parts of body injured: ☐ eye ☐ ear ☐ nose ☐ mouth ☐ tooth ☐ other part of face ☐ other part of head neck
☐ arm/wrist/hand ☐ leg/ankle/foot ☐ trunk ☐ other (specify):_____
Type of injury: ☐ cut ☐ bruise or swelling ☐ puncture ☐ scrape ☐ broken bone or dislocation ☐ sprain
☐ crushing injury ☐ burn ☐ loss of consciousness ☐ unknown ☐ other (specify):_____

First aid given at the facility: (e.g., comfort, pressure, elevation, cold pack, washing, bandaging)
_____

Treatment provided by:_____
☐ No doctor or dentist's treatment required
☐ Treated as an outpatient (e.g., office or emergency room)
☐ Hospitalized (overnight) # of days:_____

Number of days of limited activity from this incident: _____ Follow-up plan for care of the child:_____

Corrective action needed to prevent reoccurrence:
Name of official/agency notified:_____ Date:_____
Signature of staff member: _____ Date:_____
Signature of Legal Guardian/Parent:_____ Date:_____

Adapted from Pennsylvania Chapter AAP, Healthy Child Care PA, 1997 *"Model Child Care Health Policies"*

3. *Recognize what is age-appropriate for each child.* Safety precautions need to keep pace with the developmental stages of each child. It is important to be ready for the day when a child masters a new skill—for example, climbing out of the crib or opening the front door. It's equally important, however, not to assume a child is capable of handling a situation that is too advanced for him or her.

4. *Create a safe environment.* Keep a child from physical harm by removing dangers from his or her surroundings, for example, using locks on cabinets, tying up strings on blinds.

5. *Supervise children carefully.* There is no substitute for adequate adult supervision, no matter how safe the environment or situation appears to be. Know where children in your care are and what they are doing at all times.

## Age-Appropriate Safety Guidelines

To supplement this prevention plan and the household child-proofing precautions, follow these age-appropriate safety guidelines.

### AGE-APPROPRIATE SAFETY GUIDELINES

**Infants (Birth to 1 Year of Age)**

- Never leave a baby unattended on a bed, table, or other surface the baby could roll off.
- Never leave a baby in a mesh playpen with one side down.
- Always check water temperature before putting baby in it.
- Reduce the risk of choking accidents by ensuring children do not come in contact with small objects, such as buttons, balloons, toothpicks, popcorn, coins, grapes, or nuts. Always sit with a child as he or she eats. Do not prop up bottles, and do not allow a child to crawl or toddle around while eating or drinking.
- Do not give infants toys that are heavy or fragile or that have batteries or small parts.
- Supervise babies around furniture and near water.
- Never tie pacifiers (or anything else) around a baby's neck.

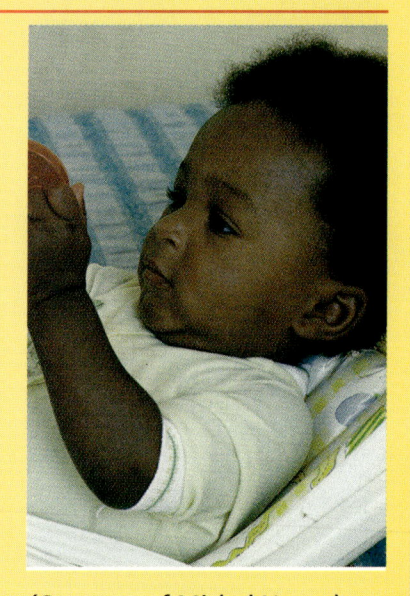

*(Courtesy of Michal Heron)*

## Toddlers and Preschoolers (Age 1 to 5)

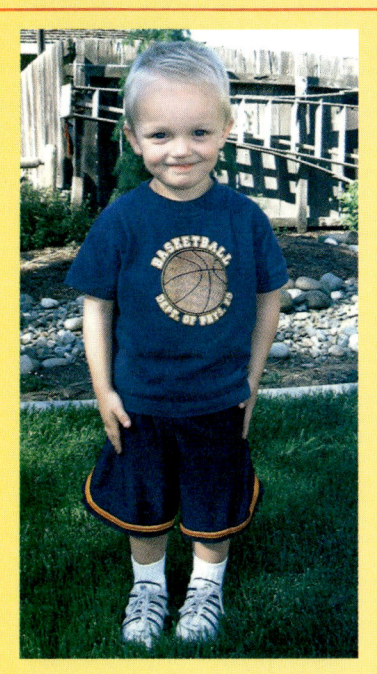

- Think ahead and be ready for what children may get into next.
- Always use safety straps on high chairs and strollers, since climbing and squirming are to be expected at this age.
- Childproof and poison-proof your home or center carefully. Dangers such as electrical outlets, stovetops, and medicine cabinets are particularly attractive to an inquisitive child.
- Inspect toys for fragility, small parts, sharp edges, projectiles, and other hazards.
- Choose nontoxic paints, markers, crayons, and so on.
- Teach preschoolers the basic principles of fire safety.
- Provide safety helmets.
- Teach young children the importance of water safety rules. Never ever take your eyes from a child near water.

## Older Children (Age 5 to 9)

- Teach children to swim.
- Teach children pedestrian safety and bicycle, scooter, and rollerblade safety.
- Show children how to use new toys safely.
- Remove all potential dangers from areas where children will probably be spending more time alone, such as bedrooms or playrooms.
- Avoid having guns in a home. If a gun must be in a home, be sure it has a trigger lock, is kept in a locked cabinet, and ammunition is locked up in a separate place.

## Children's Medical Information

Despite our best efforts, injuries will occur. When children are injured and medical attention is required, there are several things that can be done to help those providing care. After the appropriate people have been contacted (i.e. 911, parents, private physician), provide a copy of the child's medical information to EMS or emergency department staff. This information should be easy to read and at a minimum should include:

- Physicians: names and telephone numbers
- Health Plan: numbers and contact numbers
- Emergency Contacts: name and telephone numbers
- Medical Conditions: type and current treatment, allergies
- Current Medications: include over-the-counter medications

Quickly providing this information to medical professionals can help save a child's life.

## Medication Administration

Administering medication is serious business. Avoid telling children that medication "tastes like candy" or is a "treat". Once children think orange or grape or cherry flavored cold medicine is candy, it is difficult to dispel that link. Even over-the-counter medications can have serious side effects if taken in the wrong dose or mixed with other drugs. Unfortunately, children die each year from improper medication administration.

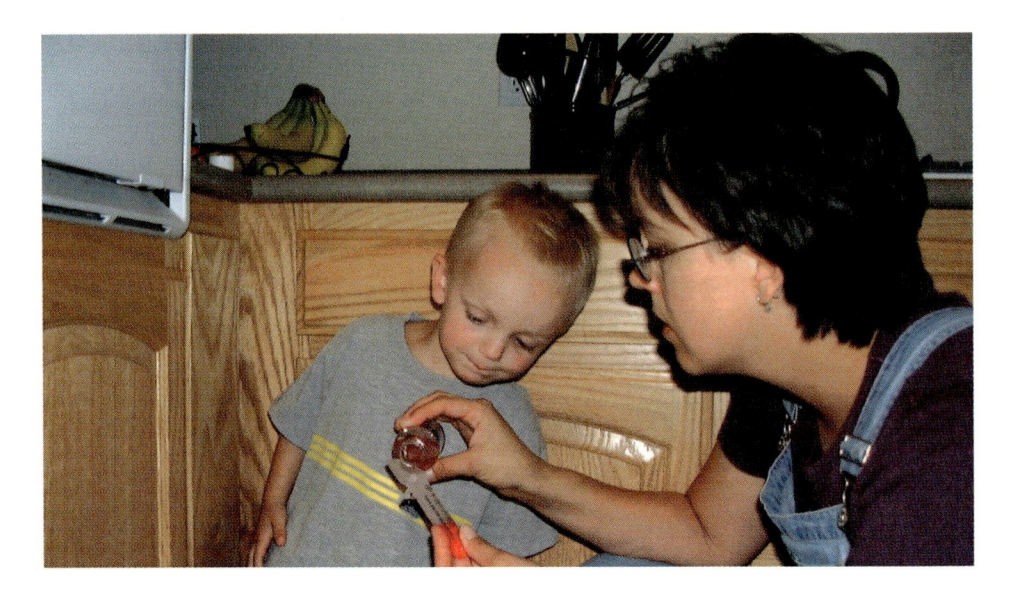

*Checking proper medication dose.*

## CHAPTER 1   Prevention, Prevention, Prevention

Childcare providers must be diligent in following their state's regulations for the administration of medication. Over-the-counter medications should only be given if a letter from the child's primary care physician is on file. Never alter the dosage on the container unless directed by a physician. ALWAYS ensure the following:

- Medication is prescribed by a licensed provider.
- Medication is in its original container.
- Medication has an expiration date, and medication has not expired.
- Medication has instructions for administration.
- The four rights are followed.
  - —Right child
  - —Right medication
  - —Right dose
  - —Right time

Be sure to store ALL medications in locations that are secured and out of reach of children.

## Basic Fire Facts

In the United States senior citizens age 70 and over and children under the age of 5 have the greatest risk of fire death. The fire death risk for children under age 5 is nearly double the risk of the average population. In 2000, the United States Fire Administration (USFA) reported that:

- The U.S. has one of the highest fire death rates in the industrialized world. For 1998, the U.S. fire death rate was 14.9 deaths per million population. Between 1994 and 1998, an average of 4,400 Americans lost their lives and another 25,100 were injured annually as the result of fire.
- Each year, fire kills more Americans than all natural disasters combined.
- Fire is the third leading cause of accidental death in the home; at least 80 percent of all fire deaths occur in residences.
- About 2 million fires are reported each year. Many others go unreported, causing additional injuries and property loss.

The following graphics show in what areas fires are most likely to start in homes and apartments.

**Fires in one- or two-story family dwellings most often start in the**

Kitchen   23.5%

Bedroom   12.7%

Living Room   7.9%

Chimney   7.1%

Laundry Area   4.7%

**Apartment fires most often start in the**

Kitchen   46.1%

Bedroom   12.3%

Living Room   6.2%

Laundry Area   3.3%

Bathroom   2.4%

## CHAPTER 1    Prevention, Prevention, Prevention

Not only is fire a childhood killer, it is a leading cause of childhood injuries. Implementing the fire-prevention techniques and guidelines below can help prevent these injuries.

- Install a smoke alarm. A working smoke alarm dramatically increases a person's chance of surviving a fire. Approximately 88 percent of U.S. homes have at least one smoke alarm. However, these alarms are not always properly maintained and as a result might not work in an emergency. Over the last ten years there has been a significant increase in the number of fires that occur in homes with non-functioning alarms.

- Teach children never to cook alone or without asking an adult.

- Turn pot handles toward the center of the stove.

- Never put anything over a lamp, like clothes or a blanket, not even when playing.

- Teach children to never touch radiators or heaters. Instruct them to always ask an adult to turn a heater on or off.

- Educate children never to stand too close to a fireplace or a wood stove. Let them know that their clothes could catch on fire.

- Teach children to never touch matches, lighters, or candles. Let them know that if they ever see matches or lighters in a room, they should tell an adult immediately.

- Establish and teach children about gathering points in case a fire occurs. Chaos is the common element during a fire. All of us can remember the fire drills we had during grade school. Fire drills are an important part of any fire safety program. Children should frequently practice exiting a home or building during a fire and how to gather at a predetermined location. You may want to identify and practice with more than one location. For example, children should meet at the front mailbox when exiting from the front of the house or center and the alley parking area if exiting the rear. Good locations typically include the mailbox, a neighbor's porch, or nearby fire hydrant. Wherever you decide to meet, make sure every child practices getting to those gathering points quickly.

*Designate gathering point in case of fire.*

Remember that fire kills and kills fast! Encourage your center staff, family, and friends to contact their local fire department for more information on fire safety programs in their neighborhoods. The benefits of fire safety programs cannot be emphasized enough. Learning how to prevent fires does save lives. For more information regarding fire safety education, visit the United States Fire Administration's website at www.usfa.fema.gov/kids.

# CHAPTER 2

# PEDISCAN CHECKLIST

## INTRODUCTION

As suggested in the last chapter, the key to successful management of childhood emergencies must include a wellrounded and realistic injury prevention program.

Checklists have proven to be one of the most successful methods used to prevent pediatric injury and should be part of any injury prevention program. Childcare providers can use the checklists to quickly scan the various areas children can enter to ensure all safety precautions have been taken and that no dangerous situations exist. Keep in mind, however, that no checklist can address all the potential problems that can exist in every home and at every facility. The PediScan checklist in this chapter should be used as a foundation; any site-specific concerns should be added to the list.

Every childcare provider should develop a systematic method of checking the childcare environment for unsafe conditions and correcting any problems before children are allowed to enter the area. As a childcare provider, your diligent and consistent efforts to prevent injuries play an important role in reducing the number of actual emergency situations that can occur. A lack of concern or unwillingness to stick to the rules can only spell future disaster.

By using the PediScan checklist in this chapter, you can improve the safety of your home or facility and reduce the risk of serious pediatric injury.

## PediScan Checklist

To assist you in developing a safe environment for children in your care, we have included a PediScan Checklist. Use this checklist as a template or guideline for what to look for when assessing children's environment for any potential troubles. The PediScan Checklist has been designed for both home and professional childcare facilities. Remember to add items that apply to your specific situation. You may need to use only certain sections of the checklist on a daily basis. You may also want to adapt the list so that you check some items daily and other items when necessary. The key to success is to establish a systematic method for checking the children's environment for all potential hazards.

### PEDISCAN CHECKLIST

| | Yes | No | |
|---|---|---|---|
| **BATHROOM** | | | Stepping stools available |
| | | | GFI outlets operational and regularly checked |
| | | | Electrical equipment unplugged and stored away from water |
| | | | Cleaning products locked and out of child's reach |
| | | | Toilet paper easily reachable by child |
| | | | Potty chairs easy to clean with bleach solution |
| | | | Toilet lids have safety latches that keep them closed when not in use |
| | | | Adequate toilets available |
| | | | Handwashing facilities with proper soaps and paper towels |
| | | | Diaper/soiled linens changed away from food preparation areas |
| | | | Changing tables have safety rails |
| | | | Biohazard trash cans open with step pedal |
| | | | Water temperature gauge set at no more than (120° F) |
| | | | Skid-proof bath mats |
| | | | Medication/cosmetics stored or locked out of children's reach |
| | | | Expired medications discarded |
| | | | Shelving high enough so children cannot reach or climb on top |
| | | | Rubber mats or abrasive treads installed inside the shower and tub |
| | | | Children never allowed to be alone in the tub |
| | | | Glass containers removed or replaced with plastic containers |

# CHAPTER 2 PediScan Checklist

|  | Yes | No |  |
|---|---|---|---|
| **HALLWAY** |  |  | Door knob covers prevent small children from entering the room altogether |
|  |  |  | Chemical cleaners stored in clearly marked containers and out of reach of children |
|  |  |  | Children not allowed to sit or play on stairs |
|  |  |  | Doorways to stairs or unsupervised areas closed and locked unless used as emergency exits |
|  |  |  | Emergency exits have easy-open latches |
|  |  |  | Safety glass used in all potential impact areas |
|  |  |  | All entrances monitored as a security precaution |
|  |  |  | Hallways and stairs frequently checked for objects that can cause a fall |
|  |  |  | Handrails installed at proper adult and child heights |
|  |  |  | Handrails installed on both right and left sides |
|  |  |  | Hallways and stairways well-lit with switches at appropriate heights |
|  |  |  | Stairway gates locked |
|  |  |  | Stairway gates either solid or with small enough holes to prevent strangulation |
|  |  |  | No accordion type gates in use |
|  |  |  | Elevated platforms include guardrails or protective barriers |
|  |  |  |     Preschool (elevated 20 inches or more) |
|  |  |  |     School age (elevated 30 inches or more) |
|  |  |  | Handrails are child hand-hold size |
| **KITCHEN/FOOD PREPARATION AREA** |  |  | Nonperishable food stored in labeled, insect-resistant metal or plastic containers with tight lids |
|  |  |  | Five-gallon buckets not accessible to children |
|  |  |  | Refrigerated medicines kept in closed container to prevent spills |
|  |  |  | Food preparation areas clean and free of cracks |
|  |  |  | Utensils and dishes clean, free of cracks, chips, and lead |
|  |  |  | Appliances and sharp or hazardous cooking utensils stored out of children's reach |
|  |  |  | ABC-type fire extinguisher mounted on wall near stove |

*continued*

## PEDISCAN CHECKLIST *continued*

|  | Yes | No |  |
|---|---|---|---|
| **KITCHEN/FOOD PREPARATION AREA** |  |  | All caregivers know how to properly operate fire extinguisher |
|  |  |  | Danger zone in front of the stove identified and off-limits to all children |
|  |  |  | Trash stored away from the stove, furnace, and hot-water heater |
|  |  |  | Stepping stool available for reaching high places |
|  |  |  | Children not allowed in kitchen during food preparation periods |
|  |  |  | Cleaning chemicals stored out of reach of children under lock and key |
|  |  |  | Chairs or stools promptly removed from kitchen area |
| **PLAY AREAS/PLAYGROUND** |  |  | Drinking water and first aid supplies nearby play area |
|  |  |  | File maintained on each piece of play equipment, including manufacturer's name and address |
|  |  |  | Records kept on equipment purchase, installation, inspection, maintenance, and approval by the Consumer Product Safety Commission and American Society for Testing of Materials (CPSC/ASTM) |
|  |  |  | Portable toys/equipment have designated storage areas |
|  |  |  | Age-specific play areas separated by distance or a physical barrier |
|  |  |  | All toys and play equipment free from pinch points, sharp edges or points, and chipped paints |
|  |  |  | Painted toys free of lead |
|  |  |  | Toys that are mouthed washed after each use |
|  |  |  | No plastic bags, balloons, latex/vinyl gloves allowed around play areas |
|  |  |  | All toys too large to be choking hazards |
|  |  |  | Toy chests have air holes and no locking mechanisms |
|  |  |  | Shooting or projectile toys not present |
|  |  |  | Rugs, curtains, pillows, blankets, and cloth toys are flame-resistant |
|  |  |  | Hinges and joints covered |
|  |  |  | Bike/tricycle riding areas separate from playing areas |
|  |  |  | Playgrounds fenced in |
| **SLEEPING AREA** |  |  | Blankets, pillows, sheets, and clothing are flame-resistant |
|  |  |  | All curtain pull strings either removed or designed for quick breakaway |
|  |  |  | All electrical outlets covered |
|  |  |  | All heater coils, heater vents, or other hot surfaces properly protected |

# CHAPTER 2 PediScan Checklist

|  | Yes | No |  |
|---|---|---|---|
| **SLEEPING AREA** |  |  | Changing tables stable with appropriate guardrails |
|  |  |  | Room lighting excludes power cords |
|  |  |  | Cribs safety approved with proper spacing between slats |
|  |  |  | Animals kept out of the sleeping area |
|  |  |  | Sleeping surfaces firm; soft bedding not accessible to infants |
| **GENERAL INDOOR AREAS** |  |  | Guns, darts, and cap pistols not kept in childcare settings |
|  |  |  | Safety covers on all electrical outlets |
|  |  |  | Electrical cords not accessible to children |
|  |  |  | Floors smooth with non-skid surfaces |
|  |  |  | Rugs skid proof |
|  |  |  | Doors easily opened from outside by a child |
|  |  |  | Security doors have panic release mechanisms |
|  |  |  | Doors in childcare areas have see-through panes so children are visible to anyone opening door |
|  |  |  | Doors have slow closing devices or rubber stoppers to prevent finger pinching |
|  |  |  | Glass doors and all full-length windows have decals at eye level for children and adults |
|  |  |  | All windows have closed permanent screens |
|  |  |  | Bottom windows lockable |
|  |  |  | Childcare setting free of toxic or lead paint |
|  |  |  | All fans have covers or guards to prevent hair or fingers from getting caught |
|  |  |  | All hot surfaces protected or include guards to prevent burns |
|  |  |  | Free standing space heaters not used in childcare settings |
| **GENERAL SAFETY GUIDELINES** |  |  | Tap water set at or below 120° F |
|  |  |  | No smoking allowed in the childcare setting |
|  |  |  | All sharp edges cushioned |
|  |  |  | Emergency lighting equipment regularly inspected and serviced |
|  |  |  | Sufficient lighting available in all areas |
|  |  |  | All childcare settings easily viewed by adults |
|  |  |  | Drawers and cupboards secured with child safety latches |

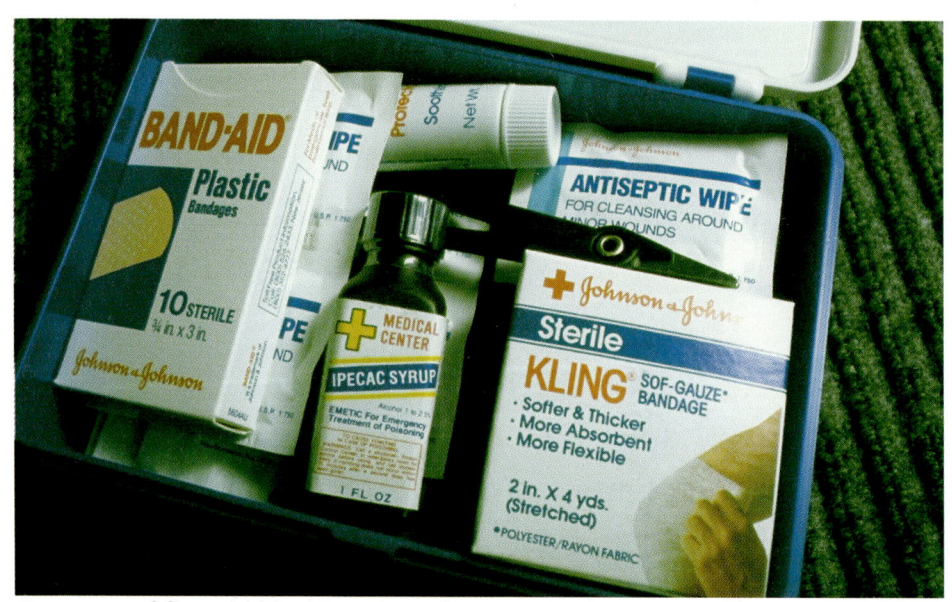

*One type of first aid kit. (Courtesy of Tony Freeman/PhotoEdit)*

## First Aid Kits

When injuries do occur, you should have immediate access to a basic first aid kit. This kit should be stocked with supplies that are appropriate for the majority of the injuries children might suffer. Stock the kit with the materials that realistically will be used at your facility. Avoid purchasing a kit that includes materials that probably will never be used. For example, one center had a first aid kit that included large amounts of old army rations! Clearly mark all kits and place them in easy accessible sites but out of reach of children. During orientation of new childcare providers, be sure they are shown the location of each first aid kit, as well as understand how to use the kit.

Regularly check each kit to ensure that it is fully stocked and ready. Be sure to check with your local or state licensing agency for a list of statutory requirements involving first aid kits. Once your kit is complete, make a contents list and place it inside the kit. This provides a quick inventory checklist when needed. A basic first aid kit should include the following supplies:

### Basic First Aid Kit
Absorbent Cotton

*Activated Charcoal (use only as directed by Poison Control Center)

Adhesive Strip Bandages (knuckles, fingertips, etc.)

Adhesive Tape (2-1" wide)

Antiseptic Towelettes

---

*Check with your local licensing agency before using any items marked with an asterisk*.

Blanket (lightweight reflective)

Butterfly Bandages

*Calamine Lotion (check state regulations)

Coins for the Pay Phone (in case cell phone not available)

Cotton-Tipped Swabs

Drinking Cups (paper or plastic)

*Eyewash (4 oz)

Flashlight (small with extra batteries)

Gloves (latex or non-latex in various sizes)

Ice Packs (instant or reusable)

Large Triangular Bandages

Measuring Cup

Measuring Spoon

Safety Pins

*Salt or Salt Tablets (for heat exhaustion), use only as physician directed

Sharp Scissors (with rounded ends)

Sterile Eye Pads

Sterile Gauze Bandages

Sterile Gauze Pads (assorted sizes, 2-2" wide)

*Syrup of Ipecac (use only as directed by Poison Control Center)

Thermometer (electronic—Tympanic)

Tweezers (to remove splinters)

Tongue Depressors

Ziploc® Plastic Bags

### Special First Aid Kits

You might consider placing the following specialized first aid kits in your care facility. However, be sure that you check with your local licensing agency before using any special medical kits. You can always get assistance from the National Poison Control Center by calling 1-800-222-1222.

- **Insect/Bee Sting Kit** (available by prescription only, for persons with severe allergic reactions)

- **Snakebite Kit** (contains a constricting band, sterile blades, and a suction device)

- **Poison First-Aid Kit** (may contain syrup of ipecac, activated charcoal, and Epsom salt). Only use under the direction of the Poison Control Center.

# CHAPTER 3
# DISASTER PLANNING

*On May 3, 1999, an F5 tornado struck central Oklahoma. Nine daycare centers were totally destroyed and 28 family care homes received serious damage. The tornado came through at 7:15 P.M. The hour was important because all the centers were vacated. What if the tornado came through at 3:00 P.M.?*

## INTRODUCTION

Being prepared when disaster strikes can save lives and reduce injury. There have been a number of disasters that have affected, or potentially affected, the care of children in either the childcare center or family home care. Developing a disaster, or emergency, plan is an essential step in providing for the safety and well being of children in childcare. This chapter provides you with the essential components of a disaster (emergency) plan, and a list of resources where you can get additional information that will assist you in preparing for a disaster incident that could affect you and the children in your care.

While this chapter focuses on plans to follow in case a natural disaster occurs, many of the guidelines are applicable for unnatural disasters, such as those resulting from terrorist attacks. In any disaster, the key to preventing injury and saving lives is preparedness.

### Determining Preparedness

Do you have a plan on how you will evacuate the children if needed or where you will seek shelter within the facility in a matter of minutes? How will the center staff care for 20–150 children of various ages and requirements? Do you have an organized method of evacuation? How will you meet the nutritional, medical, and social needs of the children in an evacuation?

Where do you begin? First, determine what types of natural disasters occur in your area: floods, tornadoes, hurricanes, or forest fires. Ask yourself the following questions to determine if you are prepared.

- Is there a local warning system?
- Do you have a designated area within your center or home to go to?
- Do you have an evacuation plan if needed?
- Do you have access to a local shelter? If not, what is location of closest public shelter?

- Do you have an identification system for the children and staff in case of separation?
- Do you have emergency notification cards on each child?
- Do you have a "Disaster Kit" to take with you if you have to evacuate?
- Have the children and the parents been taught about the plan?
- Does the local police department, fire department, and EMS know your plan of evacuation?

## Developing a Disaster Plan

Disaster planning should be a required topic discussed in every childcare setting. This topic is often overlooked because many feel that a disaster will never happen to them or in the community. Too often a disaster happens and then we realize that we should have had a plan.

The childcare center or family home should integrate its plan with the plan of the community or local neighborhood (if there is a local plan). A center or home director should begin by researching the local licensing agency, Department of Human Services, or Office of Childcare. There are few recommendations made by national associations or established standards on how to develop a disaster plan. The only recommendation is that you have one.

Your city has an office of disaster management. Contact this office and ask for any information they can provide to assist you in developing your plan, as well as for a listing of shelters that you could utilize for evacuation. Call your local fire department and invite firefighters to talk about their role in the disaster plan and how they are prepared to assist you. Local TV weather personalities will usually provide fact sheets or even come out to talk with the staff and children about weather-related disasters.

The Federal Emergency Management Agency (FEMA) provides extensive information about disasters at its website **www.fema.gov.** FEMA has also established another website **www.femaforkids.gov** for children to get information through interactive play. Both sites are excellent resources you can provide to the parents of children in your care. There is also the American Red Cross coloring book titled "Disaster Preparedness" that you can give to children to help educate them about disasters.

Children need calm, confident leadership in the face of a disaster. They can respond in many different ways to an emergency situation. Children may fear being separated from familiar surrounding and having to leave behind personal belongings. Fear, withdrawal, anxiety, and inconsolable crying are common reactions. A provider who has prepared for these reactions will be able to recognize and assist these children and manage the situation with confidence and calm. Licensing staff at your local Department of Human Services or Office of Childcare can assist you in obtaining a child psychologist to provide education regarding a child's psychological needs during disasters.

### Safe Room/Evacuation Plan

Have you established an area within your center or home that you and the children in your care can evacuate to? "Safe rooms" refer to an inside room that has no windows, and which is not part of an outside wall. When your only option is to evacuate to a safe room you must consider the size. Is it large enough to accommodate all the children and staff? Do you have items that you can use to cover your heads? Bicycle helmets or mattresses are effective. Most injuries in safe rooms occur from falling debris. Use the safe room only if evacuation is not possible. Evacuation of your center or home requires additional planning. Where do you go? A neighbor's shelter? The local school, church, or public building? This is a major part of your disaster plan. Do not take for granted that a school or other public building can accommodate you and your children. The other important thing to have in the plan is how to get to the shelter. Do you have enough transportation? Seek the help of local police, fire, and community disaster departments to help you develop this part of your plan.

### Emergency Disaster Kit

Once you have planned for moving the children to the safe room or evacuation center, you will need at least 2–6 hours of support materials, such as blankets, food, medication for some children, diapers, etc. Identification of the children is absolutely essential. Identification cards with photographs must include all the emergency contacts and special needs of the children. You can also use wristbands that give the child's name, emergency phone numbers, and special needs. Have a family day (preferably on a weekend) and invite all the children and their parents to come to the center to fill out the cards (wristbands), take photographs, and listen to a disaster plan orientation. The identification cards, or wristbands, or both, should be kept in the Disaster Kit. This kit should be updated at least every 3 months.

Besides the identification materials, the Emergency Disaster Kit should include:

- Battery-powered flashlights (extra batteries) for each provider
- Battery-powered radio (extra batteries)
- Additional first aid kit (don't rely on having enough notification time to include your center's kit)
- Cash (roll of quarters for phone calls)
- List of emergency phone numbers
- Bottled water
- Infant formula concentrate/powder and bottles

| | |
|---|---|
| Name: _____ | Parents' Name: _____ |
| SS#: _____ | Work Phone #: _____ |
| Birth Date: _____ | Physician's Name: _____ |
| Height: _____ | Physician's Phone #: _____ |
| Weight: _____ | Insurance Company: _____ |
| Address: _____ | Policy Number: _____ |
| Home Phone #: _____ | Medical Conditions: _____ |
| Childcare Facility: _____ | Medications: _____ |
| Address: _____ | Allergies: _____ |
| Facility Phone #: _____ | |

*Front and back of a child's identification card.*

- Infant diapers
- Extra set of center keys
- Blankets
- Large plastic bags
- Children's books, games, puzzles, stuffed toys, crayons, etc.
- Cell phone/pager (if available)

This is a suggested list based on the recommendations from those organizations whose resources are available to you. These organizations are listed at the end of this chapter.

## Natural Disasters

The area of the country where you reside will determine the preparations that you will have to make. Specific recommendations for each type of natural disaster are given below.

### Floods

Check with your city or county offices to determine if they participate in the National Flood Insurance Program. If your center or home is in a participating community, you live in a flood zone. They will be able to tell you what zone your center or home is in and what additional disaster plans are available for your area. Know your early warning signals and develop your plan based on your city and community guidelines.

### Hurricanes

The only advantage of hurricanes is the early warning system available through the U.S. Weather Service, local media, and the local Red Cross.

During a hurricane, your first responsibility is the safety and well being of the children. If you are advised to evacuate the area, activate your plan for notification of parents and secure the children's safety.

### Tornadoes

These powerful acts of nature do not only occur in "Tornado Alley." There have been many instances where tornadoes have struck with little warning in areas of the country seldom visited by these devastating natural disasters. Recent tornadoes in Oklahoma, Alabama, Texas, and Kansas have caused very severe and devastating damage and loss of life. Childcare centers rarely have an available "safe room" in their facility to handle the number of children they care for. Therefore the center staff should develop a plan that includes evacuation to a safe location within the community. Check with your community resources to see if there is space in a community shelter to accommodate the number of children and staff. If none are available, there are resources available that can be utilized to make your center or family home more structurally sound and safer than it is currently. These resources are listed below.

### Earthquakes

Earthquakes are not confined to just the West Coast as commonly thought. Earthquakes have been recorded in areas along the Mississippi River and in New England and the southern Appalachians. You can make your center or home safer by surveying it and determining what can be structurally changed to secure items and eliminate falling objects. You must know where your water, gas line, and electrical shut offs are located so you can turn them off. Designating a space where you can put loose items like toys and small chairs and tables can reduce the amount of falling or flying debris in the facility.

## Available Resources

The following organizations can be of assistance in helping you prepare a disaster plan so you can ensure the health and safety of the children and staff.

American Academy of Pediatrics—www.aap.org

American Red Cross—www.redcross.org

Emergency Medical Services for Children National Resource Center—www.ems-c.org

Federal Emergency Management Agency—www.fema.gov and www.fema.gov/kids

Institute for Business & Home Safety—www.ibhs.org

Insurance Information Institute—www.iii.org/individuals/disasters

# SECTION 2

# UNIVERSAL SYMBOLS TRAINING

| Chapter 4 | Scene Safety | 26 |
| --- | --- | --- |
| Chapter 5 | Standard Precautions | 29 |
| Chapter 6 | Initial Assessment | 32 |
| Chapter 7 | Ongoing Assessment | 36 |
| Chapter 8 | Activation of the Emergency Medical Services (EMS) System | 40 |
| Chapter 9 | Basic Life Support: Rescue Breathing (Artificial Ventilation) | 42 |
| Chapter 10 | Basic Life Support: Cardiopulmonary Resuscitation | 49 |
| Chapter 11 | Shock | 55 |
| Chapter 12 | Soft-Tissue Injury | 58 |
| Chapter 13 | Musculoskeletal Injury/Immobilization | 65 |
| Chapter 14 | Spinal Precautions | 69 |
| Chapter 15 | Oxygen Application | 72 |

# CHAPTER 4

## SCENE SAFETY

### LEARNING OBJECTIVES

*After completion of the chapter, the childcare provider should be able to:*

- List dangerous situations that could occur in their own childcare environments.
- Demonstrate the ability to determine and report basic mechanism of injury and nature of illness information.
- Demonstrate how to check an emergency environment for safety hazards.

### SYMBOL INDEX

## INTRODUCTION

As a childcare provider, one of your primary concerns during all emergency situations must be your own personal safety and the safety of those around you. You must always first evaluate the scene and determine if it is safe to enter before making direct contact with the child. Failure to evaluate the scene will put you at extreme risk for becoming a patient yourself. Violent crime scenes, electrical hazards, toxic spills, fires, floods, auto crashes, a collapsed structure, explosions, and uncontrolled power equipment are just a few examples of potentially dangerous scenes. Think about situations in your home or facility that could present as a dangerous scene. Never enter into a scene that is dangerous. If you are injured while attempting to enter an unsafe scene you will only further complicate the situation.

## Mechanism of Injury/Nature of the Illness

Once the scene is safe, the fire is out, the electricity is turned off, or the assailant has fled, the childcare provider must make a quick determination of the cause of the injury by determining what happened. The cause is commonly called the **mechanism of injury.** The mechanism of injury suggests the forces involved and clues to possible injuries. After an auto crash, for example, a variety of collisions and impacts between organs within the body can take place depending on the mechanism of injury involved. These in turn can cause a number of hidden injuries. As you try to determine the mechanism of injury, think about the forces involved, the body parts affected, and all possible injuries. Once you have this information, you can better estimate potential injuries or problems before they become obvious—or deadly.

Some emergency situations involve illness rather than trauma. Gathering basic information regarding the complaint, medical history, or other pertinent information helps determine what is called the **nature of the illness.** This information is gathered by asking a sick child questions that are clear and to the point. If a child is unconscious or otherwise unable to communicate, you should question any available bystanders.

Information related to either the mechanism of injury or nature of illness is vital to you and to EMS or other health care professionals who will be treating the child. This information must be shared with the EMS system (911 dispatch, paramedics) as well as the emergency department staff. If you have trouble remembering details under pressure, write down the information.

### DANGER!

Danger! Always take the time to evaluate the emergency scene before you proceed with child care. With experience, you will begin to trust your instincts about whether a scene is safe to enter. EMS veterans call this their "street sense" or "sixth sense." The one time you forget this life-saving step could be the last!

*EMS dispatch center responds to 911 calls.*

## Steps  Scene Safety Evaluation

Use the following guidelines to evaluate a scene for safety.

- Obtain as much information as possible about the emergency situation from bystanders if you were not nearby. If there is any possibility of danger, do not enter the scene. Not entering a scene can be very difficult, especially if you can see or hear an injured child. If violence is involved, activate local law enforcement (911).

- Communicate with the child from a safe distance. Provide reassurance and explain that help is on the way.

- If you are specifically trained and have the proper emergency equipment to handle dangerous scenes, then enter and render aid to the child.

### Real-Life Response

The windstorm seemed especially fierce this afternoon. You are gathering the children from the backyard when suddenly a power line from a nearby pole snaps and lands on the ground. The line is hot and sparks fly everywhere. The power line has fallen between you and several children who are playing on the nearby playground equipment. They are startled by the noise and begin to cry and call out. In the chaos you watch a small boy fall from the top of the slide. What will you do?

# CHAPTER 5 — STANDARD PRECAUTIONS

### LEARNING OBJECTIVES

*After completion of the chapter, the childcare provider should be able to:*
- List the ways infectious diseases are spread to childcare providers.
- Recognize emergency situations requiring the use of standard precautions.
- Demonstrate how to use basic personal protective equipment.

### SYMBOL INDEX

## INTRODUCTION

Any disease that can be passed from one person to another is called a communicable, or infectious, disease. Every childcare provider must be concerned about coming into contact with a child's bodily fluids. Childcare providers can be infected by direct contact (touching blood) or indirect contact (breathing airborne droplets). In the last several years, the AIDS (HIV) epidemic, hepatitis B (HBV) infections, and tuberculosis (TB) outbreaks have heightened awareness about the need for protection against infectious diseases.

In response to these serious developments, the Centers for Disease Control (CDC) have developed policies designed to protect childcare providers. These policies are collectively called "standard precautions." Standard precautions are also referred to as universal precautions or body substance isolation. As a general rule, the CDC encourages all childcare providers to take standard precautions whenever it might be

# CHAPTER 5  Standard Precautions

*Handwashing may be the most important way of preventing infection.*

possible that the provider could come in contact with a child's bodily fluids. Standard precautions must be taken regardless of the child's appearance, medical problem, or social status. Do not make judgments about children's disease potential based on the way they look, dress, or act.

## Personal Protective Devices

Basic common sense, inoculations, and personal protective devices are usually sufficient to protect you against the risks of infection. Handwashing is perhaps the simplest and easiest protection against infection. Disposable medical gloves should be used whenever there is a possibility you might come in contact with a child's bodily fluids. Remember, however, that some children are highly allergic to latex. In such cases, it is necessary to use non-latex (nytral) gloves. When appropriate, additional devices such as face shields, masks, and gowns should

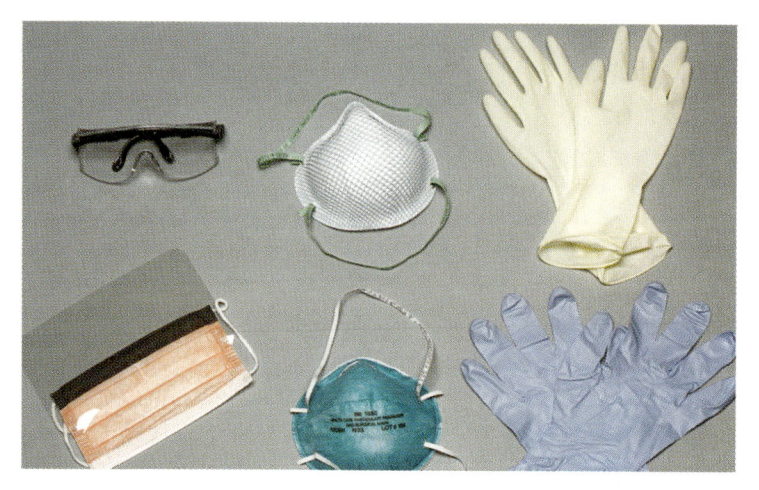

*Standard precautions, or body substance isolation, equipment used to prevent exposure to infectious diseases.*

# CHAPTER 5  Standard Precautions

## DANGER!

Once personal protective equipment has been used, it must be disposed of properly. If the protective material is soaked and dripping body fluids, it must carefully be placed in a specially marked biohazard container. The container must be disposed of according to local or state laws.

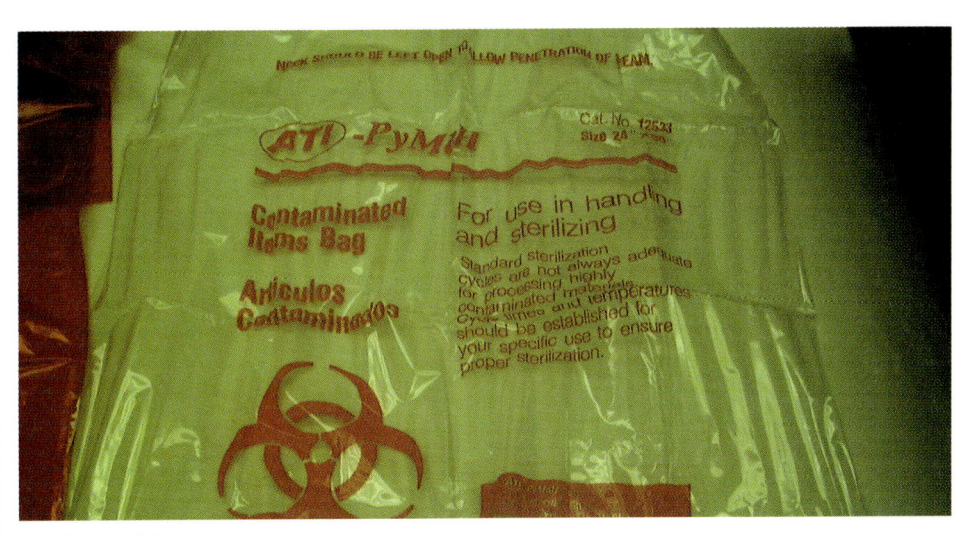

*Biohazard bag.*

be utilized. Every childcare provider should frequently practice using standard precautions when reviewing first aid skills. This practice will be invaluable during real emergencies. Contact your local medical supply company for information about personal protective equipment.

## Steps  Standard Precautions

1. 
2. Locate and don appropriate personal protective equipment (latex gloves, mask, gown).
3. Dispose of soiled materials in a proper container (biohazard bag).

### Real-Life Response

Next week marks your second year of managing a small childcare facility. Just as you begin reflecting on all your experiences, you hear a loud cry coming from just around the corner. As you approach, you notice a small boy holding his chin, and blood is streaming down his fingers. The boy is crying loudly and jumping up and down. You just began caring for this child the previous week, and this is the second time he has injured himself. He states he ran into the corner of the table while playing. He continues to bleed and the blood begins pooling on the floor. The first aid kit is across the play area in the kitchen. What will you do?

## CHAPTER 6 — INITIAL ASSESSMENT

### LEARNING OBJECTIVES

*After completion of the chapter, the childcare provider should be able to:*

- *List the emergency conditions that require the completion of an initial assessment.*
- *Recognize the importance of the initial assessment.*
- *Demonstrate the steps in the initial assessment.*

### SYMBOL INDEX

### INTRODUCTION

In every safe emergency situation, a childcare provider must first be concerned with immediately correcting all life-threatening conditions. Only when these conditions have been corrected, can the childcare provider then turn his or her efforts toward a child's less serious problems. To assist the childcare provider in checking for potentially life-threatening problems, an initial assessment was developed. When a child in your care is injured or becomes ill you must immediately conduct an initial assessment. This assessment should take no longer than 60 seconds to complete. During this initial assessment, you first assess child's airway, then breathing, then circulation, and finally serious hemorrhage (massive bleeding). To remember the exact steps in the initial assessment, memorize the letters A, B, C, and H.

CHAPTER 6　Initial Assessment　　33

# S T E P S

**INITIAL ASSESSMENT**

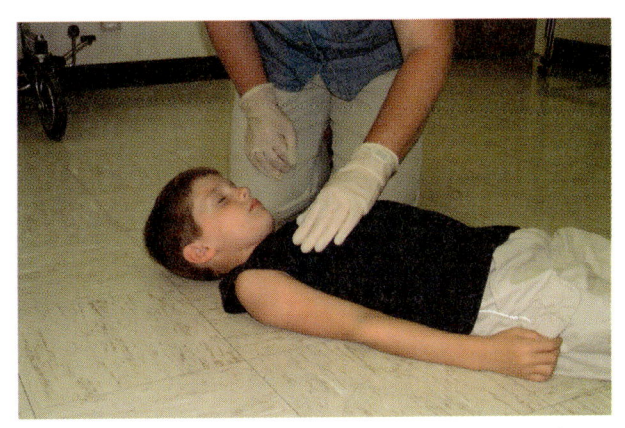

1. Determine responsiveness (shake and shout "Hey, hey are you okay?).

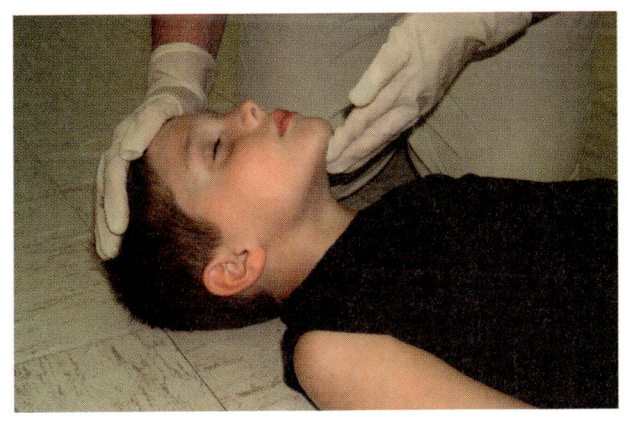

2. A = Airway. Open the airway using the head-tilt chin-lift.

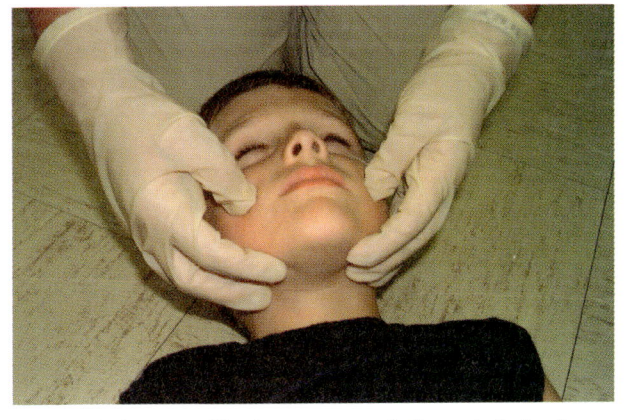

For children suffering potential neck injuries use the jaw-thrust maneuver.

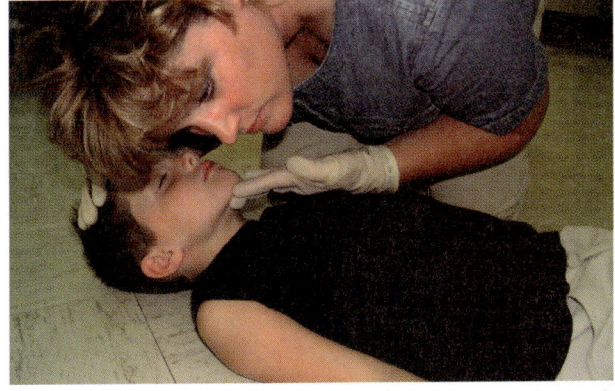

3. B = Breathing. Look for the rise and fall of the chest. Listen for breath sounds from the mouth and/or nose. Feel for chest movement and breath flow of air against your cheek.

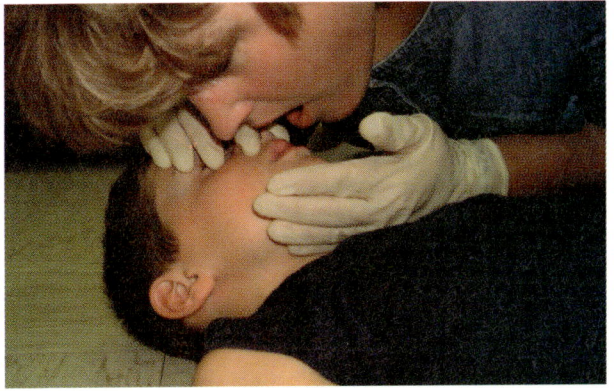

If the child is not breathing, begin rescue breathing. (Steps are covered in Chapter 9.)

*continued*

## CHAPTER 6 Initial Assessment

# STEPS

### INITIAL ASSESSMENT continued

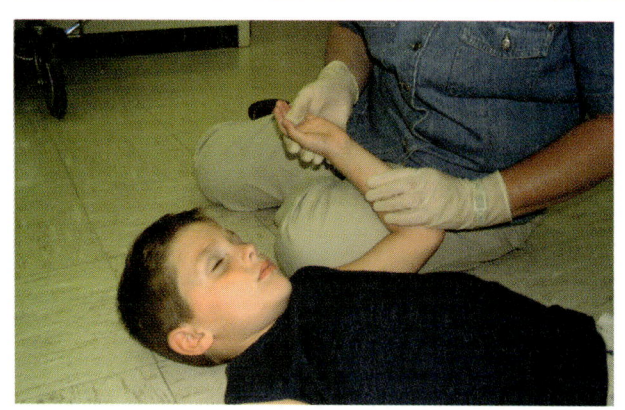

**4.** C = Circulation. Check for signs of circulation (normal breathing, coughing, or movement).

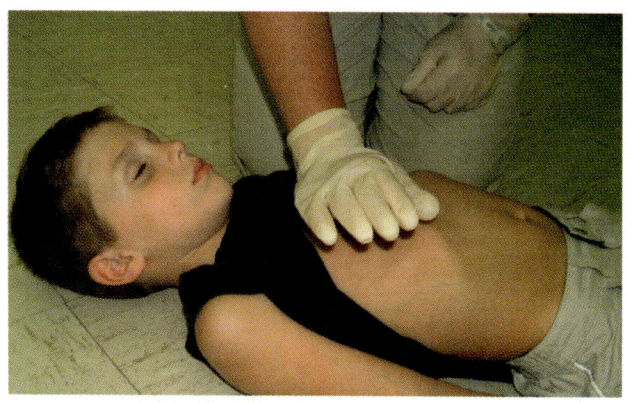

**5.** If there are no signs of circulation, begin chest compressions and rescue breathing. (These steps are detailed in Chapter 10.)

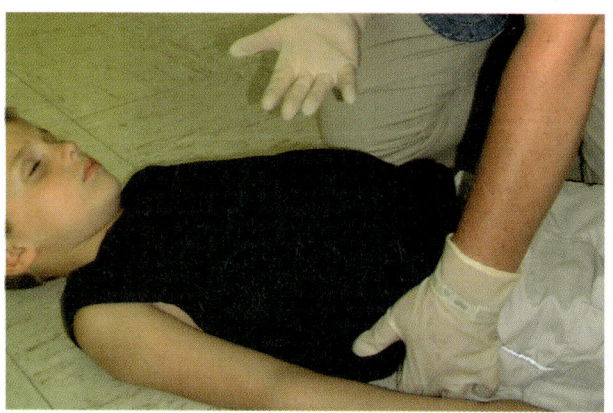

**6.** H = Hemorrhage (massive bleeding). Quickly run your gloved hands completely over and under the child; periodically check your gloved hands for evidence of massive bleeding.

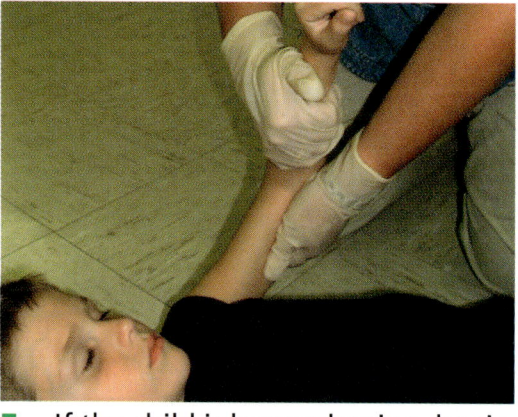

**7.** If the child is hemorrhaging, begin bleeding control through applying direct pressure, elevation, and pressure points. (See Chapter 12 for detailed steps.)

**8.** Immediately activate the Emergency Medical Services (EMS) system (dial 911) if the child does not respond or is unconscious.

### FYI

If the child or infant is lying on his or her stomach, gently roll the child/infant onto his or her back. If you suspect a neck injury, get help and carefully roll the patient onto his or her back. Attempt to maintain an imaginary straight line between the child's nose and navel while turning the patient.

### FYI

The American Heart Association no longer suggests that lay rescuers be taught to check for a pulse during the A,B,C,H sequence. Instead they suggest that the rescuer should examine the patient and look for "signs of circulation," which include normal breathing, coughing, or movement. Research shows that lay rescuers have a difficult time locating the correct palpation point of a pulse.

A childcare provider must recognize that during the first few minutes of any childhood emergency one must focus on managing a child's airway, breathing, and circulation. Remember that without an open and clear airway, breathing stops, and eventually the heart stops.

### Real-Life Response

Susan has been working as a professional childcare provider for more than six years. You arrive at the playground just in time to see Susan who is about to begin treating a child who was reported to be having a seizure. The child is shaking uncontrollably and is not responding to his surroundings. Susan is obviously upset and unsure of what to do. What suggestions might you offer her?

## CHAPTER 7

# ONGOING ASSESSMENT

### LEARNING OBJECTIVES

*After completion of the chapter, the childcare provider should be able to:*

- List the emergency conditions requiring the completion of an ongoing assessment.
- Recognize the importance of the ongoing assessment.
- Demonstrate the steps required during an ongoing assessment.

### SYMBOL INDEX

## INTRODUCTION

The ongoing assessment is a thorough hands-on physical exam that should be performed on any injured child. However, the ongoing assessment should be performed only **after** all life-threatening conditions associated with a child's airway, breathing, circulation, and bleeding have been managed appropriately. Minor injuries, usually found during an ongoing assessment, always take a second seat to those injuries associated with the ABCH.

### Ongoing Assessment Strategies

During the ongoing assessment try to determine the child's chief complaint (the main cause of pain or illness). Then find out what caused the injury or illness and look for medical alert medallions.

# CHAPTER 7 Ongoing Assessment

Frequently recheck the child's condition using the initial assessment. Remove the child's clothing if it interferes with your assessment or treatment. While performing the ongoing assessment, constantly communicate with the child. This is the easiest way to determine any changes in a patient's airway, breathing, or circulation. Any trouble with the ABCHs usually affects the child's ability to communicate, cry, or remain conscious. If you notice a change in the status of the child's A, B, C, or H, IMMEDIATELY stop the ongoing assessment and correct the problem.

During the ongoing assessment, assess the body for any injury. Look for things like scrapes or cuts, bruising, broken bones, unusual deformity, rigid or hard skin, tenderness, swelling, and punctures. Report all your findings to the appropriate medical authority.

Make a note of any injuries or abnormalities that you find while performing the ongoing assessment. These injuries can be treated after completion of the ongoing assessment. Treatment of specific injuries or illnesses will be covered in later chapters.

> **FYI**
>
> Some situations may require that the childcare provider conduct the ongoing assessment toe-to-head rather than head-to-toe. If the childcare provider is not known by the child, starting at the feet and working toward the head may be less threatening to the child.

# STEPS

## ONGOING ASSESSMENT

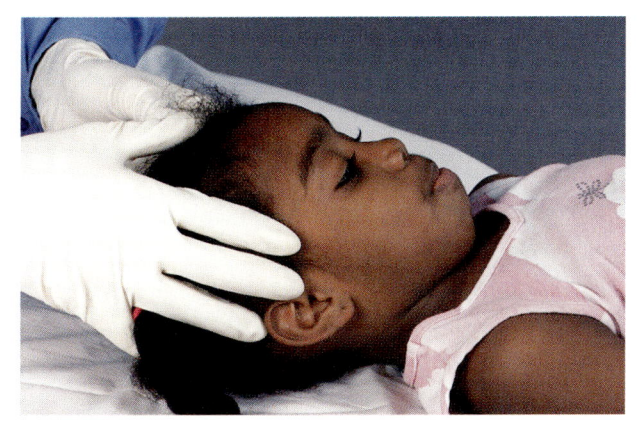

**1.** Carefully feel the head and face for injuries.

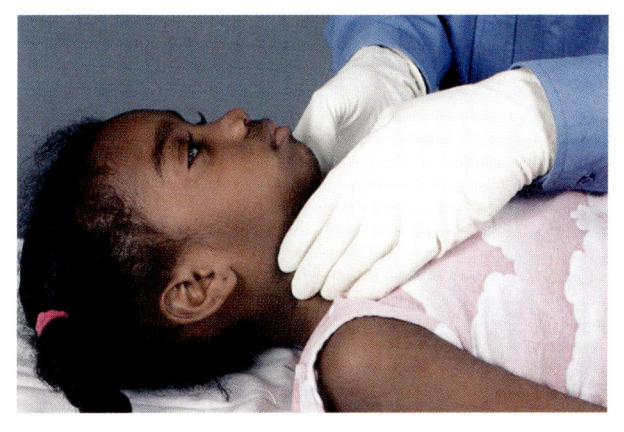

**2.** Look at the neck for obvious injuries.

**38** ■ ■ ■ **CHAPTER 7** Ongoing Assessment

**ONGOING ASSESSMENT** *continued*

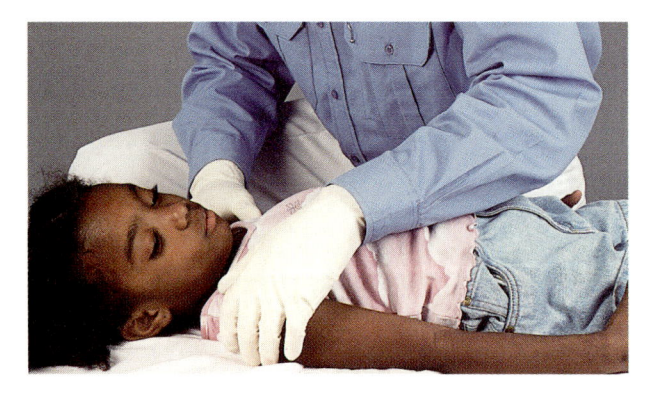

**3.** Feel the shoulders.

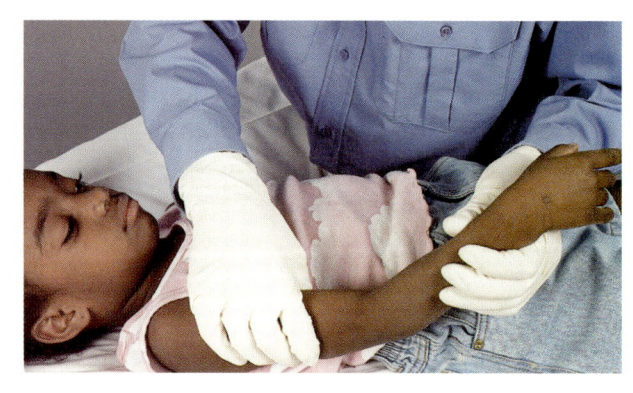

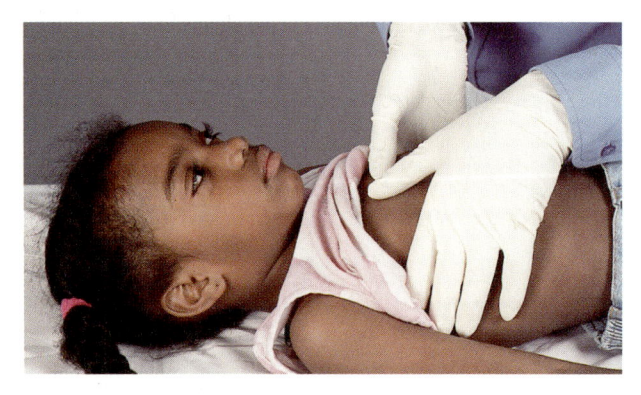

**4.** Feel the arms.

**5.** Feel and look at the chest. Look especially for any deformity to the chest or open wounds.

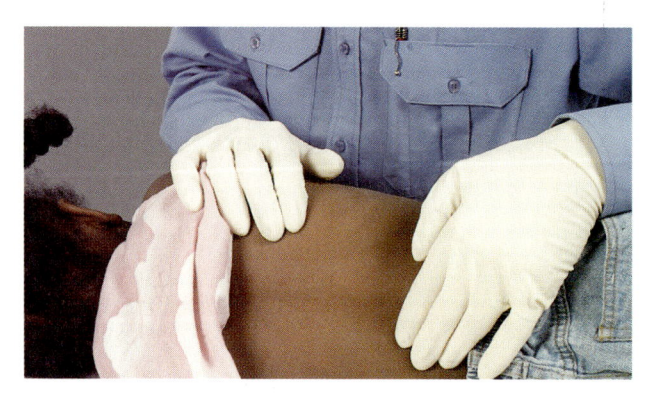

**6.** Feel the back.

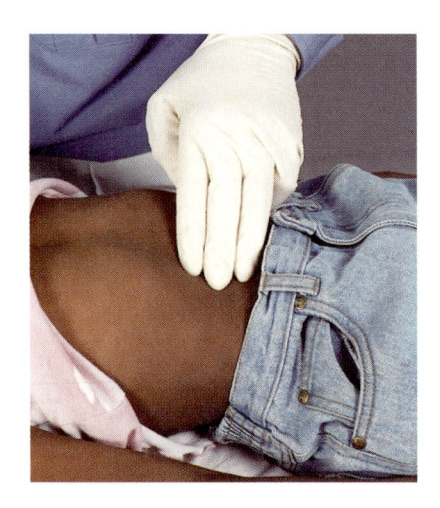

**7.** Feel the abdomen.

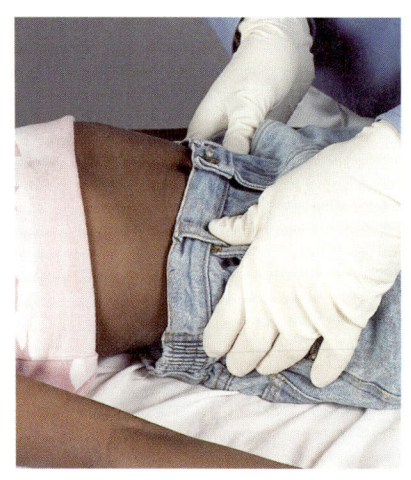

**8.** Feel the hips.

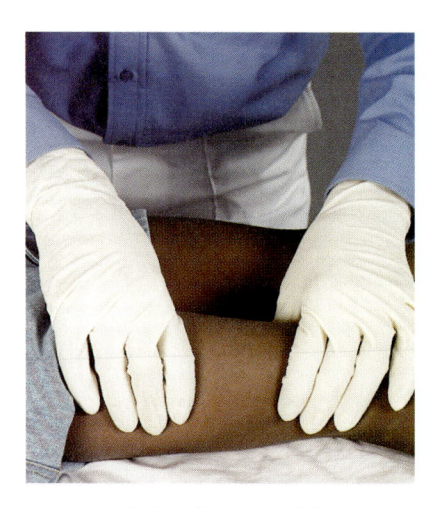

**9.** Feel the legs, ankles, and feet.

# DANGER!

In situations involving falls, head injuries, back injuries, or unconsciousness, make sure that you move the child as little as possible. A child with a head or back injury should only be moved if absolutely necessary to save his or her or your life.

### Real-Life Response

Recess is always a busy time for teachers and with the recent rainy weather the children are especially energetic. As you monitor the yard, Chan, an eight-year-old boy, comes to you holding his neck. He says he tripped and struck his head on the sidewalk. Chan is answering your questions appropriately. There is a large abrasion across his forehead. He is complaining of neck pain and discomfort in his right elbow. Describe how you would assess Chan to determine the extent of his injuries.

# CHAPTER 8

# ACTIVATION OF THE EMERGENCY MEDICAL SERVICES (EMS) SYSTEM

## LEARNING OBJECTIVES

*After completion of the chapter, the childcare provider should be able to:*

- *Demonstrate the procedure for EMS activation.*
- *Describe the importance of early activation of EMS.*

## SYMBOL INDEX

## INTRODUCTION

A serious emergency is any injury or illness that affects the airway, breathing, circulation, or bleeding. Whenever a serious emergency occurs, quick activation of the Emergency Medical Services (EMS) system by calling 911 is critical. The earlier the access to the EMS system, the less time you will be without professional help!

### Activating the EMS System

In most areas, dialing 911 or some other emergency numbers will put you in contact with the EMS dispatch center. Post these emergency contact numbers next to or directly on the phone. Be prepared to listen carefully, speak clearly and slowly, and answer key questions. Key questions may include:

## DANGER!

Never hang up after dialing 911 until directed to do so by the Emergency Medical Dispatcher. Dispatchers are trained to help you handle the situation until additional help arrives.

*Dispatch Center.*

- What is the medical emergency?
- What is your calling location?
- Where is the child located?
- Is the child breathing?
- What have you done for the child?

Our experience is that pediatric injury or illness occurs when people least expect it. To better prepare for emergency situations, we suggest that you carry a working portable or cell phone while caring for children. Having to leave an injured child in order to search for a phone can be extremely frustrating and time-consuming, resulting in the delay of emergency care.

### Real-Life Response

You have taken a small group of children on a short walk down to the large oak tree located near the back fence. Just as you begin to sit down under the shade of the tree, one of the children runs up to you and screams that he has been stung by a bee. His face and neck are swelling and small white patches are appearing on his arms and hands. You run toward the house and arrive in the kitchen, short of breath and dizzy. As you begin to dial 911, you realize that you will have a hard time speaking. What could you have done to improve this situation?

# CHAPTER 9

# BASIC LIFE SUPPORT: RESCUE BREATHING (ARTIFICIAL VENTILATION)

## LEARNING OBJECTIVES

*After completion of the chapter, the childcare provider should be able to:*

- Describe the steps to determine the breathing status of an infant or child.
- Describe the steps for rescue breathing (artificial ventilation) for an infant or a child.
- List the rates of rescue breathing for an infant or a child.
- Describe the steps for treatment of an infant or a child who is choking.

## SYMBOL INDEX

## INTRODUCTION

The number one cause of cardiac arrest in infants and children is respiratory arrest. Therefore, every effort must be made to maintain an open and clear airway when providing emergency care for pediatric patients. You must know the steps to properly manage problems with the airway and breathing in children.

As you learned in Chapter 6, your first action during the initial assessment is to assess and manage the airway. If the infant/child is breathing, you continue the initial assessment while constantly monitoring the airway

# CHAPTER 9  Basic Life Support: Rescue Breathing

until EMS arrives. If during your initial assessment you find the infant/child is <u>not</u> breathing, you must take immediate action. That action is rescue breathing, or artificial ventilation.

Rescue breathing provides the infant/child with enough of an oxygen supply to sustain life until EMS arrives to provide advanced treatment. The steps for rescue breathing are very similar for infants (one year old or less) and for children (one to eight years old). However, there are two differences—one is in how the airway is opened and the other is in how to give rescue breaths. These differences are noted below.

## Rescue Breathing

Rescue breathing is only accomplished when the infant/child is conscious or shows signs of circulation (normal breathing, coughing, or movement). Remember, the idea behind rescue breathing is to fill the infant/child's lungs with air from your breaths. Your breaths should be careful and slow, with just enough air to raise the child's chest wall. Always call for help, and activate EMS early.

## Steps  Rescue Breathing

1. 🏠
2. ☣
3. ABC

4. Open the airway. First, lay the infant/child on a hard surface, such as the floor, table, changing table.

   **Infant:** Use the head-tilt chin-lift maneuver to place the infant's head in the neutral position. It is very important that you only tilt the infant's head back so that the nose is pointing straight up, as shown below. If you push the infant's head too far backward, this will block the airway.

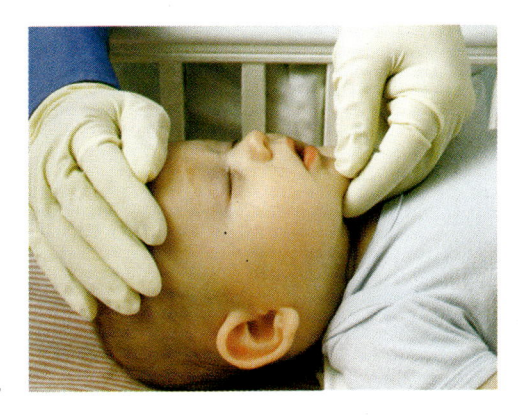

*Head-tilt-chin-lift maneuver—infant.*

## CHAPTER 9 Basic Life Support: Rescue Breathing

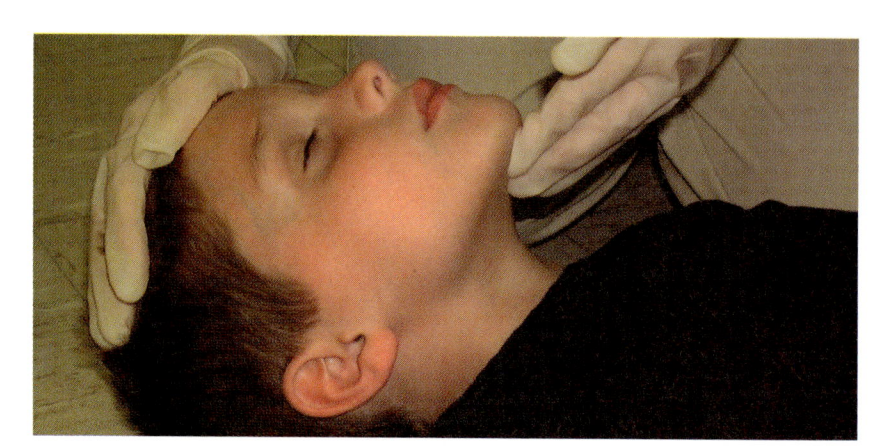

*Head-tilt-chin-lift maneuver—child.*

**Child:** Use the head-tilt chin-lift maneuver when opening the airway of a child.

5. Check for breathing. **Look** for rising of the chest or abdomen. Place your ear next to the infant/child's mouth and **listen** for breathing. Can you **feel** any breath against your cheek? If there are no signs of breathing go to number 6 . . .

6. **Infant:** Cover the infant's mouth and nose with your mouth. Form a tight seal. Puff (like blowing out a candle) into the infant's nose and mouth.

   **Child:** Since a child's nose/mouth area is too large for you to form a tight seal over it, pinch the child's nostrils closed. Then with your mouth form a tight seal over the child's mouth. (Use a barrier device if available). Breathe into the child's mouth enough to see the child's chest rise.

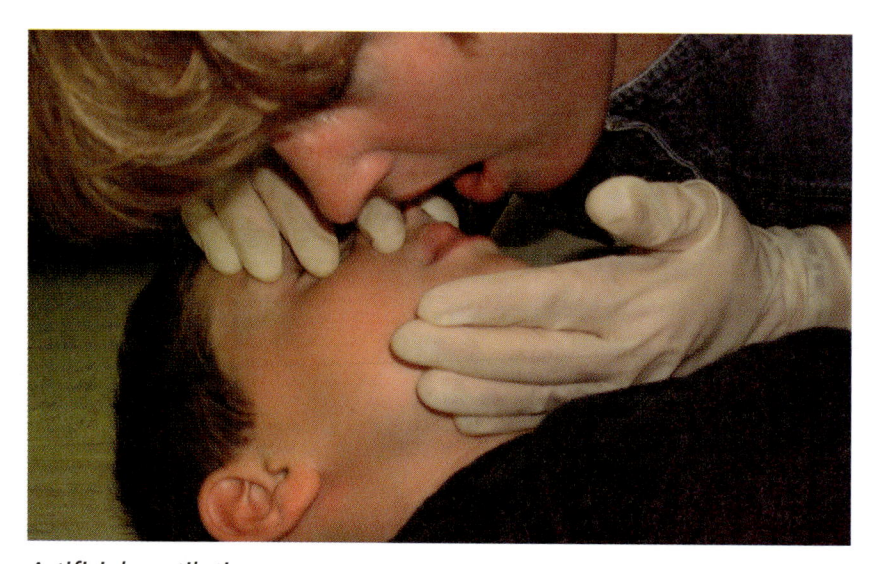

*Artificial ventilations.*

7. As long as the infant/child is not breathing, give one breath every three seconds. Count: One, Two, Three, Breath. Continue to breathe for the infant/child until EMS arrives and takes over the treatment.

8. Check circulation status.

## Foreign Body Airway Obstruction (FBAO): Choking

In an earlier chapter, we discussed injury prevention and the risk of children choking on objects. Since infants explore with their mouth, everything they handle will eventually end up there. A foreign-body airway obstruction is very serious and requires prompt and accurate intervention by you as a childcare provider.

There are two types of foreign-body airway obstruction—partial and complete. *A partial airway obstruction* allows the infant/child some limited air movement. In a *complete airway obstruction,* NO air is able to enter or exit the airway. THIS IS A LIFE-THREATENING EMERGENCY! The steps to be taken in handling a choking emergency differ for infants and children. Therefore they are discussed separately.

### Steps Partial Obstruction—Conscious Infant

In a partial obstruction, the infant may be making sounds and you may actually hear the infant breathing. You may hear sounds like wheezing or high-pitched sounds that lead you to believe that there is something caught in the infant's throat. If you hear such sounds, take quick action. Do not panic, however. Infants have powerful gag reflexes. In most cases the object will be expelled without your help. If the obstruction is not relieved naturally or the obstruction becomes complete, take the actions for a complete airway obstruction given below. Early activation of EMS should be considered, since a partial airway obstruction can quickly become a complete obstruction.

### Steps Complete Airway Obstruction—Conscious Infant

In a complete airway obstruction, the infant cannot make sounds because no air is able to enter or exit the airway. Follow these steps.

1. Immediately call out for help. If someone responds, have them call 911 or the local emergency response telephone number.

2. Place the infant face down on your outstretched arm as shown on the next page. With the heel of your hand give five back blows between the infant's shoulder blades. Each blow should be followed with increasing force until the object is dislodged or five back blows are delivered.

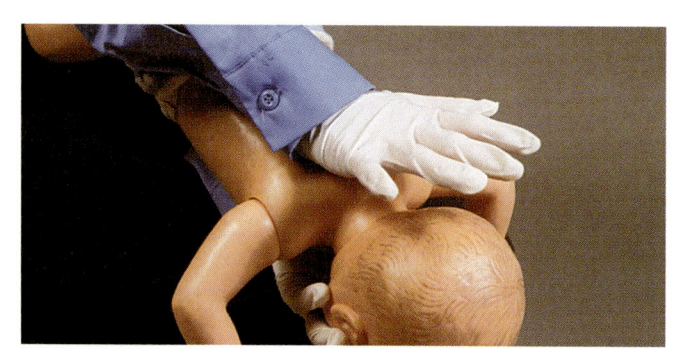

**46**  CHAPTER 9  Basic Life Support: Rescue Breathing

*Back blows.*

3. Turn the infant over onto his or her back, with head down. Make sure the infant is in a head-down position to help dislodge the obstruction. With two or three fingertips give the infant five chest thrusts.

4. Reassess the infant's airway. Look into the infant's mouth. If you see anything and can reach it, remove it. If you cannot see any object, do not put your fingers into the infant's mouth.

5. If the object is not dislodged, continue the series of back blows and chest thrusts. If the infant loses consciousness before EMS arrives, you must initiate CPR as described in Chapter 10.

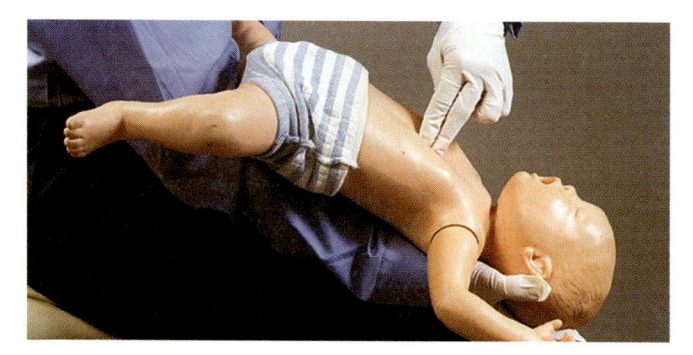

*Chest thrusts.*

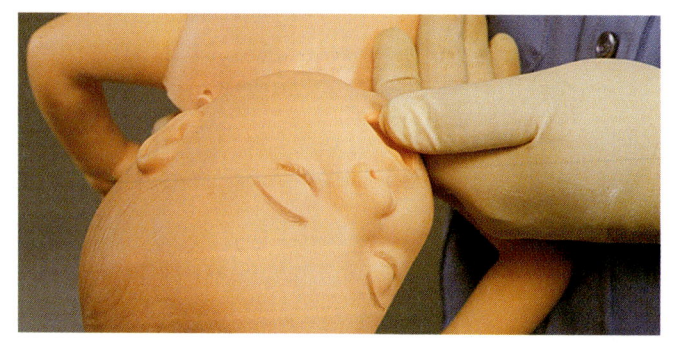

*Reassess airway.*

## Steps  Partial Obstruction—Conscious Child

Children have very active or aggressive gag reflexes and usually dislodge an object without any intervention. Reassure and coach the child in his or her attempts to naturally dislodge the object. Monitor the child until the object is coughed up or the child can no longer forcefully cough or talk. This indicates the obstruction is complete. Follow the steps for a complete airway obstruction given below.

## Steps  Complete Obstruction—Conscious Child

1. Immediately call out for help. If someone responds, have them call 911 or the local emergency response telephone number.

2. If the child is unable to respond, tell the child you are going to help remove the object.

3. Quickly stand behind the child or sit the child in your lap facing away from you. Wrap your arms around his or her waist. Support and stabilize yourself to hold the child's weight against you.

4. Place the thumb side of one fisted hand against the child's abdomen between the navel and where the lower ribs join the breastbone (xiphoid process).

5. Use quick upward thrusts, pushing inward and upward on the abdomen to cause pressure under the diaphragm. Continue the thrusts until the object is removed, the child loses consciousness, or EMS arrives to take over.

6. If the child loses consciousness before EMS arrives, place the child on a hard surface (floor or table) and begin CPR as described in Chapter 10.

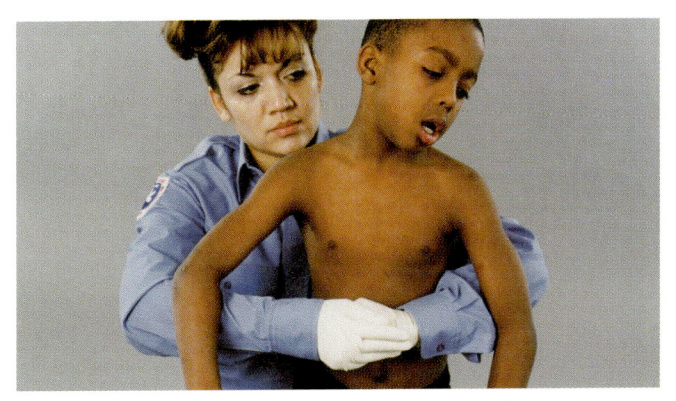

*Giving abdominal thrusts to conscious child.*

**48** | **CHAPTER 9** Basic Life Support: Rescue Breathing

### Real-Life Response

As you are cleaning up lunch trays, out of the corner of your eye you see a young boy standing up and clutching his throat. He is unable to talk and looks very anxious. What will you do?

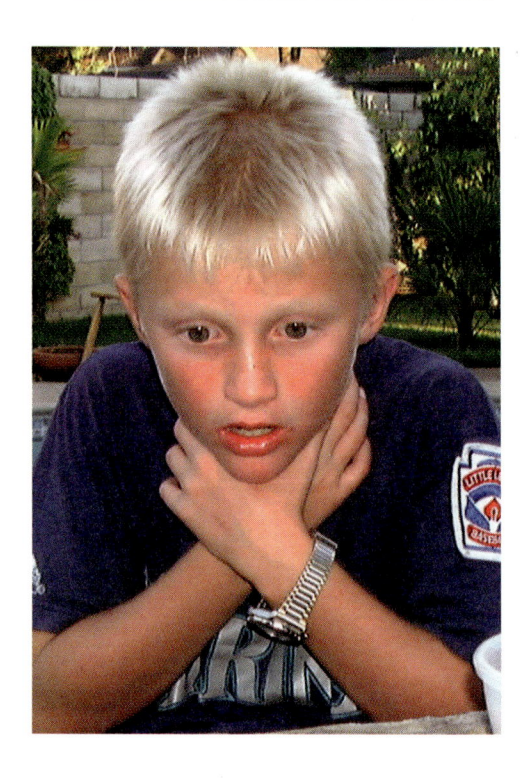

# CHAPTER 10

## BASIC LIFE SUPPORT: CARDIOPULMONARY RESUSCITATION

### LEARNING OBJECTIVES

- *Discuss the "Phone First/Phone Fast" procedure for infants and children.*
- *List the rates of artificial ventilations, ratios for chest compressions, and depth of compressions for infants and children.*
- *Demonstrate cardiopulmonary resuscitation techniques for infants and children.*

### SYMBOL INDEX

## INTRODUCTION

For several years, bystanders have been saving countless lives using cardiopulmonary resuscitation (CPR). *Cardio* refers to the heart, and *pulmonary* refers to the lungs. *Resuscitation* refers to a set of skills designed to restart the heart and lung functions after they have stopped.

Realistically, your chances of having to perform CPR are minimal. However, if the occasion arises, early CPR can make a difference between life and death. CPR involves two basic skills—giving artificial ventilations and performing chest compressions. These skills are easy to learn. If practiced often, they are also easy to recall. You have already learned half the skills—how to give artificial ventilations—in the previous chapter.

## CPR and Bloodborne Pathogens

As stated in Chapter 5, standard precautions should be used during all first aid or CPR situations. During resuscitation events, patients commonly vomit and expose the rescuer to various bodily fluids. If available, gloves and a properly sized pocket mask or face shield should be used.

## The Chain of Survival

The American Heart Association has identified a chain of events that improve any cardiac arrest patient's chance for survival. This chain of survival has four links:

- early access
- early CPR
- early defibrillation
- early advanced care

As a childcare provider your focus is on the first two links. A guideline called "Phone First/Phone Fast" is part of the early access link in the chain of survival. The "Phone First" applies to adult victims. Once you determine that the adult victim is unresponsive, not breathing, and shows no signs of circulation, activate the 911 system. The "Phone Fast" guideline applies to infants and children. If an infant or child is unresponsive, not breathing, and shows no signs of circulation, it is extremely important that you provide one minute of CPR and then activate the EMS system.

It is essential that infants and children receive at least one minute of CPR so that time without oxygen is decreased.

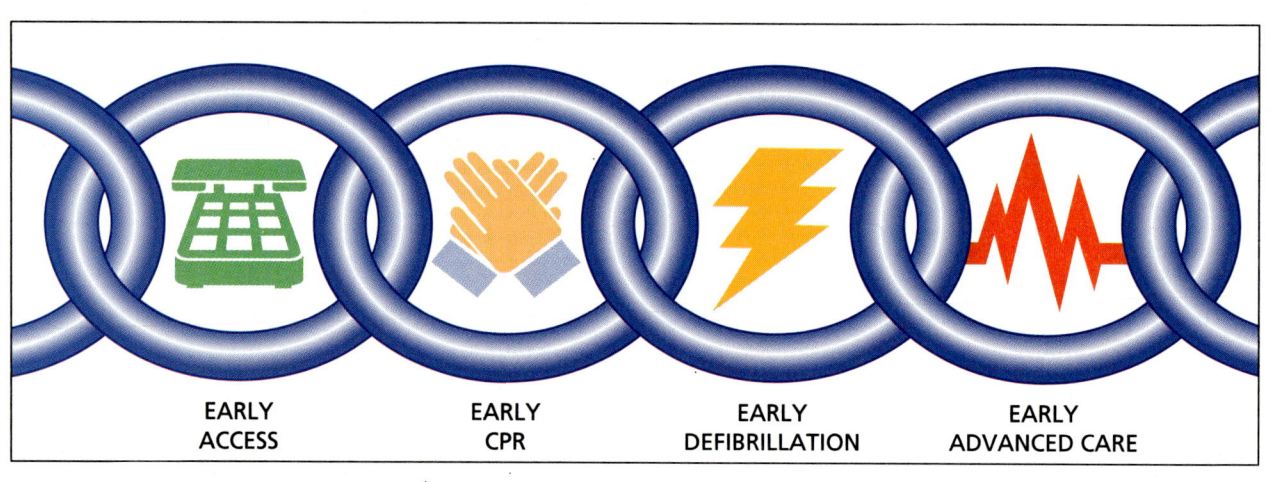

*Chain of survival.*

CHAPTER 10   Basic Life Support: Cardiopulmonary Resuscitation       51

> **FYI**
>
> The American Heart Association has recently changed the standard for lay-person CPR. The 2000 standard no longer recommends that the lay-rescuer check for a pulse to check for circulation. Assessing the patient for "signs of circulation"—normal breathing, coughing, and movement—is the only step that is required to determine if the patient requires chest compressions.

## Steps  Cardiopulmonary Resuscitation

The treatment steps for providing compressions differ for infants and children. The differences are highlighted below. As in all emergency situations, you should first complete a scene size-up to ensure your safety, the patient's safety, and the safety of those responding to help. Immediately after the scene size-up, take standard precautions and begin these steps.

1. Determine responsiveness by shaking and shouting — "Are you OK?"

2. 

3.  If the child is not breathing, provide two (2) rescue breaths.

4. Check for signs of circulation. Is the child moving? Is the child making any sound (coughing)? If no signs of circulation are present, begin CPR.

5. Begin chest compression treatment steps.

   **Chest Compressions—Child**
   You must first use the correct hand placement. Incorrect hand placement on the patient's chest increases the risk for injuries

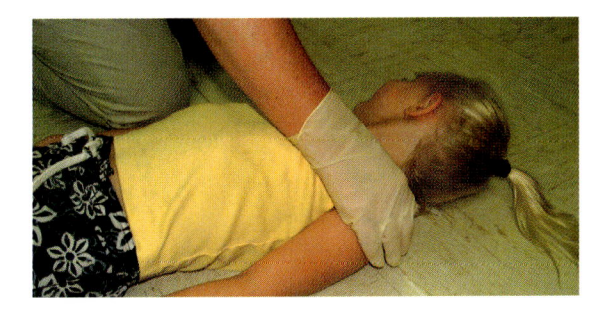

*Determine responsiveness.* 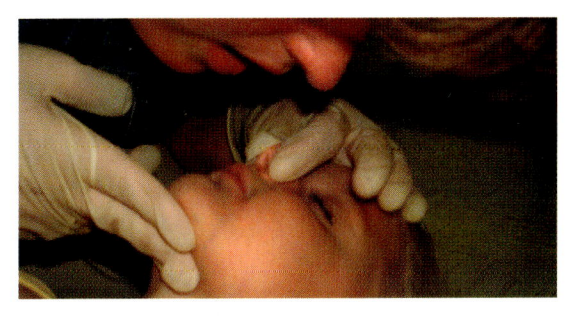                 *Provide two (2) rescue breaths.*

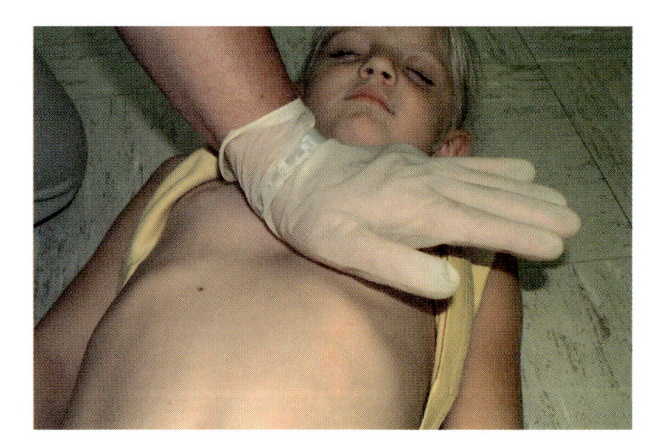

**CHAPTER 10**  Basic Life Support: Cardiopulmonary Resuscitation

*Proper hand placement for giving compressions to child.*

to the chest wall and internal organs and decreases the effectiveness of chest compressions. Follow these steps.

**1.)** First, expose the child's chest by opening the shirt or raising it up to the shoulders.

**2.)** Kneel beside the child at the chest level and run you fingers up along the rib cage.

**3.)** Find the area where the ribs join the breastbone. This is the xiphoid process. Keep your finger on this location and place the heel of your other hand above your finger as shown above. Your hand should now be in the correct position for compressions. This proper placement of your hand prevents you from compressing on the xiphoid process and breaking it off.

**STOP! Practice locating the correct position for hand placement on a child or a child manikin.**

**4.)** With your arm extended and locked on the child's chest, place your other hand on the child's forehead to keep the airway open.

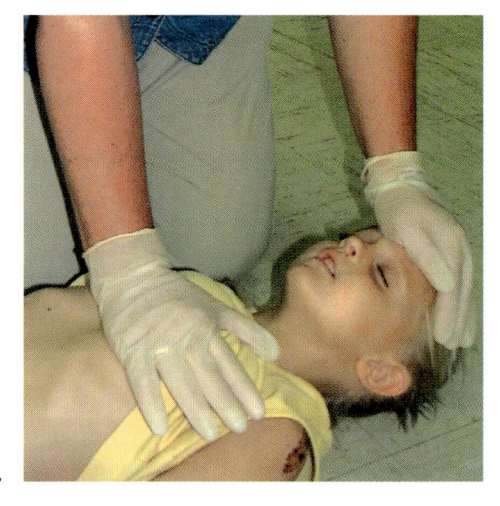

*Giving chest compressions to child.*

# CHAPTER 10    Basic Life Support: Cardiopulmonary Resuscitation    53

## DANGER!

DANGER! If you ever lose direct contact with the child's chest wall or your hand slips off the chest wall, you MUST stop chest compressions and find the correct hand position before continuing.

**5.)** Begin compressions. The depth of compressions for a child is 1-1$\frac{1}{2}$ inches. This is approximately $\frac{1}{3}$ to $\frac{1}{2}$ the total depth of the chest wall. Give 5 compressions, then 1 ventilation. Count One, Two, Three, Four, Five, Breath.

### Chest Compressions—Infant

**1.)** First expose the infant's chest.

**2.)** Place the infant face up on a flat, solid surface. Draw an imaginary line between the two nipples. Place your index finger directly on this line in the center of the infant's chest. Your middle finger and ring finger should also be in the center of the chest directly below your index finger.

**3.)** Keep your index and middle finger on the infant's breastbone. Your fingers should be over the lower third of the infant's breastbone.

**4.)** Begin compressions. Give 5 compressions, then 1 ventilation. The depth of compressions for an infant is $\frac{1}{2}$-1 inch.

*STOP! Practice locating the correct finger position on an infant or infant manikin.*

The American Heart Association recommends a compression rate of at least 100 compressions per minute for the child and the infant. For a newborn infant the rate is 120 compressions per minute. Obviously compressions must be performed faster than one per second. To meet the requirements of 100 compressions per minute, you will have to perform the cycle of 5 compressions to 1 ventilation 20 times in a minute. Practice performing compressions on a doll or pediatric manikin. Have a friend time your compression rate over a minute.

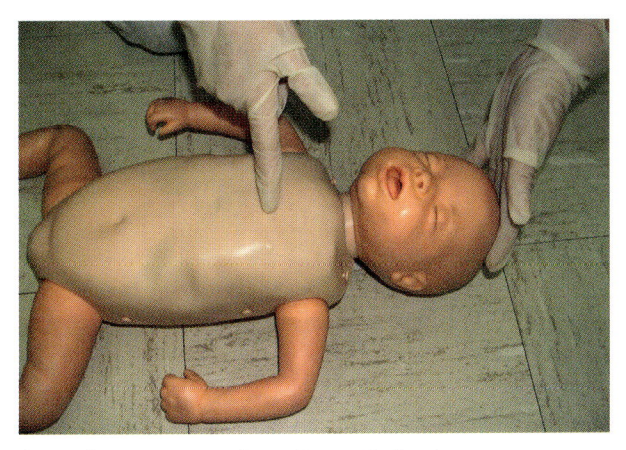

*Locating compression site on infant.*

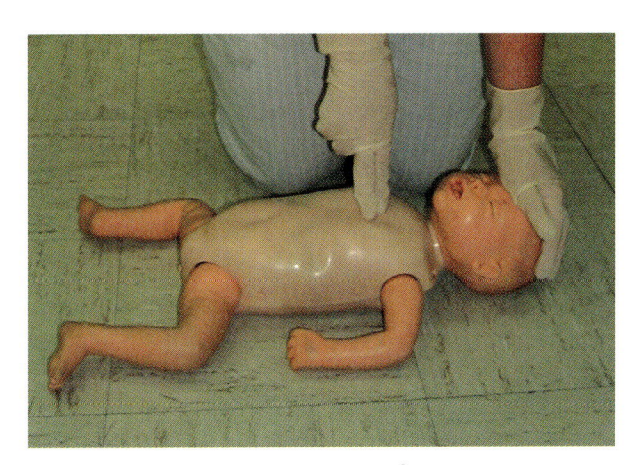

*Giving chest compressions to infant.*

You should perform one minute of CPR (20 cycles of 5 compressions/1 ventilation) and then reassess the child/infant's breathing and signs of circulation. If the child shows signs of improved consciousness such as moaning, coughing, or moving, immediately stop. If not, give one ventilation and begin the compressions/ventilation sequence again. After each set of 20 cycles, check for signs of breathing and circulation. Continue until EMS arrives.

## Common Problems During CPR Performance

As you practice your CPR skills, check for the following common problems, and practice to correct them.

- Incorrect hand/finger position
- Incorrect depth of compressions
- Failure to maintain tight seal around mouth of child or mouth and nose of infant
- Too much force used during ventilations
- Failure to maintain an open airway
- Failure to activate EMS early

## Two-Person CPR Techniques

In many emergency situations, more than one childcare provider will be involved. In CPR events, two people can perform the resuscitation skills simultaneously. One person performs chest compressions, while the other person performs the artificial ventilations. The compression ventilation ratio remains at 5:1. When either of the childcare providers becomes tired, he or she should ask for a change, which should take place at the end of the next cycle. Prior to the exchanging of positions, begin with a breath and end with breath.

### Real-Life Response

After three-year-old Lucia was left in your care this morning, you noticed her acting "different." Her parents had taken her to the doctor last night and she was given antibiotics for an inner ear infection. She was cranky, but she fell asleep shortly after lunch. After about an hour, you check on Lucia and notice immediately that she appears pale and her lips have a blue tinge. As you shake her gently to wake her up, she is unresponsive and is not breathing. What is your next step?

# CHAPTER 11 SHOCK

### LEARNING OBJECTIVES

*After completion of this chapter, the childcare provider should be able to:*

- List the various causes of shock in children.
- Describe the link between blood pressure and fluid loss.
- Demonstrate proper treatment for shock in children.

### SYMBOL INDEX

## INTRODUCTION

Shock is defined as the inadequate circulation of blood to vital body organs. There are many different causes of shock. However, this chapter focuses on shock caused by fluid or blood loss (hypovolemic shock), shock that is a result of infection (septic shock), and shock caused by an allergic reaction (anaphylactic shock).

### Types of Shock

*Hypovolemic shock* begins when the body loses fluids through external or internal bleeding, uncontrolled vomiting or diarrhea, or prolonged sweating. After enough fluid loss, organs in several body systems begin to function incorrectly. The heart has trouble pumping, the kidneys and liver have trouble filtering, and the brain struggles to send messages.

During *septic shock*, which is caused by massive infection, the body loses fluid internally as the blood vessels start to leak. As with

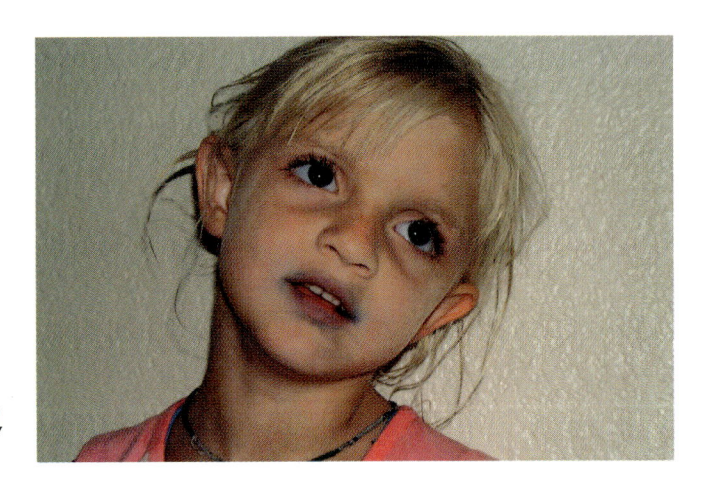

*Child with cool, pale skin.*

hypovolemic shock, the body begins to run out of fluid inside the vessels designed to keep blood pressure stable.

*Anaphylactic shock* is caused by a severe reaction to a medication, insect sting, or a substance that the person swallows, inhales or comes in contact with. In this type of shock, the blood vessel walls lose their ability to remain constricted. While very little fluid leaks from the vessels, vessel diameters become so great that the heart is unable to maintain adequate blood pressure.

As the body continues to lose fluid or the blood pressure falls to dangerously low levels, a deadly cycle of self-preservation begins. The body reduces the flow of blood and oxygen to parts of the body deemed less important. For example, the fingers, toes, and abdomen receive less blood than usual. Signs and symptoms of shock begin to appear. The pediatric patient will become confused, restless, or agitated. The skin may turn cool, pale, and moist. These are early signs of shock that indicate that the brain is not receiving an adequate oxygen supply.

## Steps Shock Treatment

Each type of shock requires specific advanced treatments. However, you can provide important basic treatment for all types of shock until EMS arrives.

1. 2. 3.

4. Elevate legs approximately 8–12 inches.

5. Prevent heat loss and maintain normal body temperature.

6. Do not give any food or drink.

CHAPTER 11   Shock   57

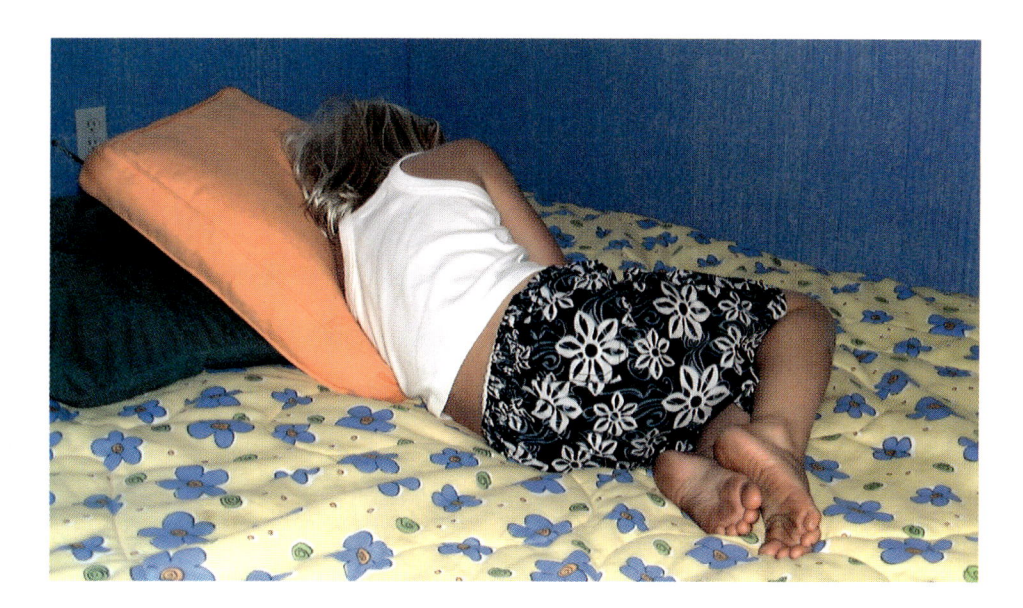

### Real-Life Response

The day-care center has been a busy place all day as every child excitedly prepares for the holiday vacation. You are looking forward to the break as well. Earlier this morning, a staff member reported that little four-year old Shawiana was not feeling well. She reported that the girl had a bad case of diarrhea and was vomiting all morning. Shawiana's parents were notified and her father stated he would pick Shawiana up at approximately 3:30 P.M. At 2:00 P.M. you check on Shawiana who is napping with the rest of her group. She is restless and cool to the touch. You notice that she is slow to respond, and her skin color is pale. Shawiana appears to be breathing faster than normal. Other staff members report to you they have not been able to control Shawiana's vomiting and diarrhea. What actions will you take immediately?

# CHAPTER 12

# SOFT-TISSUE INJURY

### LEARNING OBJECTIVES

*After completion of this chapter, the childcare provider should be able to:*

- *Describe how to reduce the possibility of disease transmission when treating a soft-tissue injury.*
- *Describe signs and symptoms of both external and internal life-threatening bleeding.*
- *Demonstrate how to control external bleeding using direct finger and hand pressure, elevation, and pressure points.*
- *Demonstrate the proper treatment for an amputation.*

### SYMBOL INDEX

## INTRODUCTION

As a childcare provider, it's likely the most common type of injuries you will treat are those to soft tissue, or the skin. The emergency treatments for soft-tissue wounds are generally easy to perform. Proper emergency care for soft-tissue wounds can have a significant impact on the overall outcome for the infant or child.

Soft-tissue wounds range from simple abrasions to complete amputations. Many soft-tissue injuries will bleed freely, especially those involving the face or scalp. The risk of exposure to bloodborne diseases increases significantly when treating actively bleeding soft-tissue injuries. Soft-tissue injuries may appear severe and cause tremendous concern. However, it is important to maintain focus on the child's airway,

# CHAPTER 12  Soft-Tissue Injury

breathing, and circulation. Soft-tissue injuries can be cared for at the hospital even several hours after the injury. In comparison, a blocked airway can kill in just a few minutes.

## Danger Signals

Bleeding which is "squirting" from a wound or which is severe enough to be obvious during the initial assessment should be controlled immediately. This type of bleeding, if left uncontrolled, can quickly lead to more serious medical problems.

Bleeding into the airway must also be immediately controlled. If blood enters the airway, it can make its way to the stomach and cause nausea and vomiting. This, in turn, can make it difficult to maintain a clear and open airway. In order to drain blood or other fluids from the airway, place the victim on his or her side in what is known as the "recovery position" if head or neck injury is not suspected.

In most cases of simple external bleeding, bleeding will stop within a few minutes. This is because blood binds to itself, or clots, and the blood flow slows or stops. In some rare instances, children can have medical conditions that inhibit this natural clotting process.

As a general rule, all open wounds should be covered to reduce the risk of infection. Although gauze bandages are preferred, other clean materials like a pillow cover, shirt, or towel can be used temporarily to cover a wound.

## Types of Soft-Tissue Injuries

Childcare providers often want to know how to judge when a soft-tissue injury is severe enough to warrant calling 911. While no hard and fast rule is available to answer this question, the bottom line is whenever you feel the injury is severe enough to require immediate physician attention or the bleeding cannot be controlled, activate 911. Determining if a laceration will require stitches depends on the

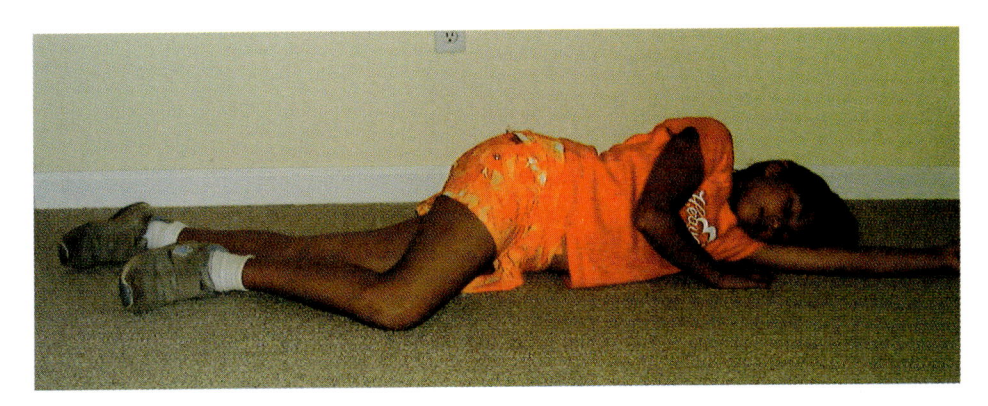

> **DANGER!**
> Always be alert for possible airway obstruction in the infant or child lying on his or her back. Saliva and vomit commonly pool in the airway. If necessary, quickly and carefully turn the child on his or her side to maintain a clear airway.

*Recovery position.*

# CHAPTER 12 Soft-Tissue Injury

location and size of the injury. The care of soft-tissue injuries depends largely on the type of wound involved. Types of soft-tissue injuries include:

Contusion (bruising or bleeding under the skin)

Laceration (incision or cut of the skin)

Abrasion (destruction of the top layers of the skin)

Punctures (penetrations to the skin causing internal tissue damage)

Avulsion (skin is torn, usually leaving a flap of tissue)

Amputation (complete separation of a body part from the body

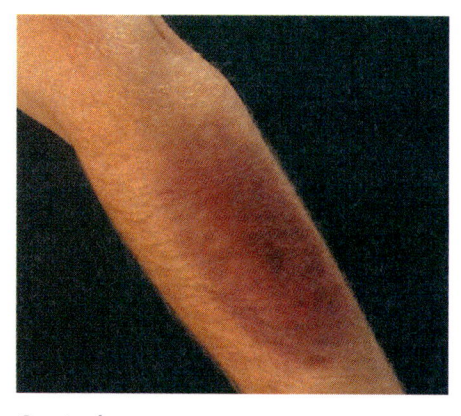

Contusion.

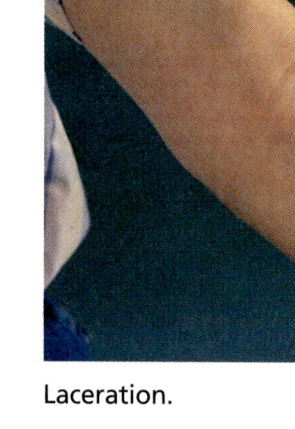

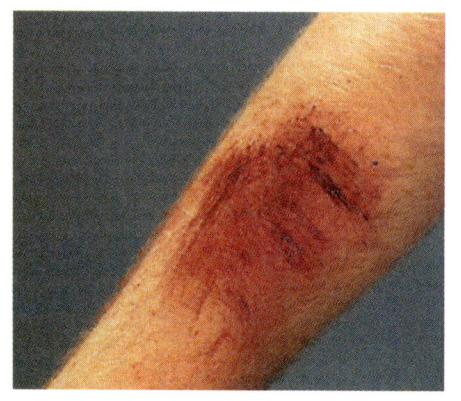

Laceration.

Abrasion.

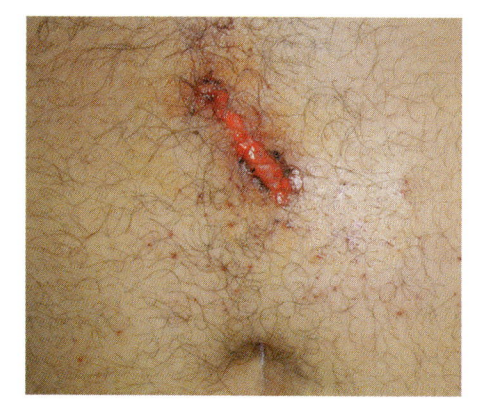

Puncture.

## Soft-Tissue Injury Treatment

In the first few minutes after the injury of soft tissue, the basic treatment is similar. Special attention must be given the patient's airway, breathing, and circulation in spite of the child's pain and anxiety level.

The basic actions for treating the majority of external soft-tissue wounds include: direct pressure, elevation, and pressure points, which are explained on the next two pages.

## Steps   External Bleeding/Soft-Tissue Injury Treatment

1. [biohazard icon]

2. [ABCH icon]

3. If the patient's wound is hemorrhaging (massive uncontrolled bleeding), immediately apply direct pressure over the wound site. With a gloved hand, apply finger pressure directly over the wound area. If a piece of clean gauze is available, place it between your hand and the wound. If the wound involves the mouth or nose, do not allow the child to spit out the blood. Have the child lean forward and let the blood drain. Allowing spitting increases the risk of exposure to bloodborne diseases for the childcare provider.

4. [step 2 icon] Treatment you continue to deliver depends on the mechanism of injury and the type of soft-tissue wound.

5. First, apply firm direct pressure over the wound (strong handshake pressure is usually best) for at least ten minutes. Place a clean material over the wound, such as a towel, large bandage, gauze, or a clean shirt.

6. Elevate the wounded area above the heart level, if possible. If you suspect broken bones, splint the area prior to elevation (See Chapter 13).

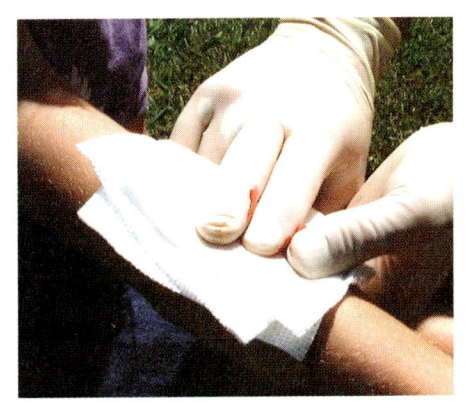

*Bleeding control—direct pressure.*

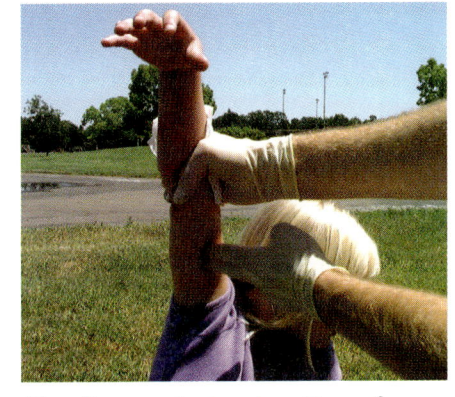

*Bleeding control—elevation of wounded area.*

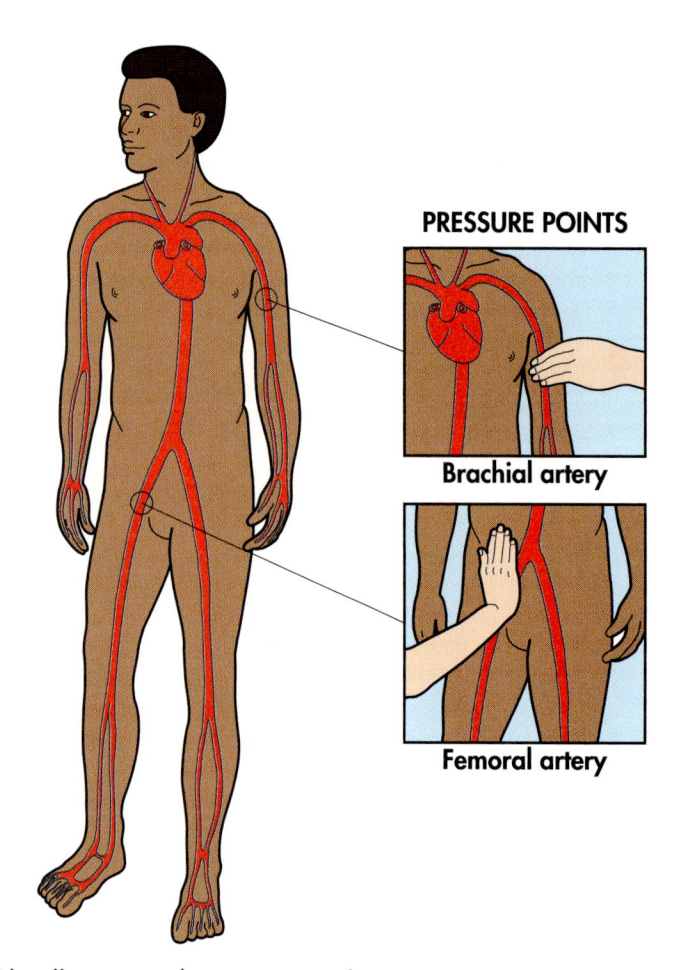

**62** ■■■ CHAPTER 12　Soft-Tissue Injury

**PRESSURE POINTS**

Brachial artery

Femoral artery

*Bleeding control—pressure points.*

7. Use pressure points if bleeding continues. Pressure points are specific locations on the body were large blood vessels lay next to bone. Compressing the blood vessel against the bone reduces the supply of blood to that area and below it.

8. If you haven't already done so, activate 911.

9.  [ABCH] Frequently reassess.

If a patient has an avulsion, place the skin flap back in the proper location prior to applying direct pressure. Then continue treatment as with any soft-tissue injury. Consider wrapping a self-adhesive bandage around the wound to control bleeding.

# CHAPTER 12  Soft-Tissue Injury

## DANGER!

Treat the child's airway, breathing, and circulation first and the amputated parts second.

Although rare, an amputation may occur. Follow the same treatment steps for any other soft-tissue wound. Apply direct pressure to the stump and locate the amputated part(s). Clean the amputated part of large debris and then place it in a moist cloth. Place in a sealed plastic bag. Place this sealed bag on top of a second bag filled with ice. Do not place the amputated part in direct contact with ice and never pack it in ice.

## Internal Bleeding

Bleeding inside the body is usually caused by ruptured blood vessels, blunt trauma, decreased blood clotting capabilities, or serious fractures. Minor internal bleeding usually results when a child is struck by or hits an object, which causes a small amount of tissue damage underneath the skin. Such injury eventually turns into a simple bruise. For example, if a child is struck by an object around the eye, some time later a black eye will develop. It is bleeding underneath the skin around the eye that causes this bruising. More serious internal bleeding can be life-threatening. Internal bleeding is often not recognized until serious complications begin to take place. The signs and symptoms of serious internal bleeding include the following.

- Bruises
- Pain
- Nausea and vomiting
- Thirst
- Discoloration
- Swelling

- Cold and wet skin
- Shortness of breath
- Anxiety
- Restlessness
- Decreased awareness
- Bleeding from any body opening

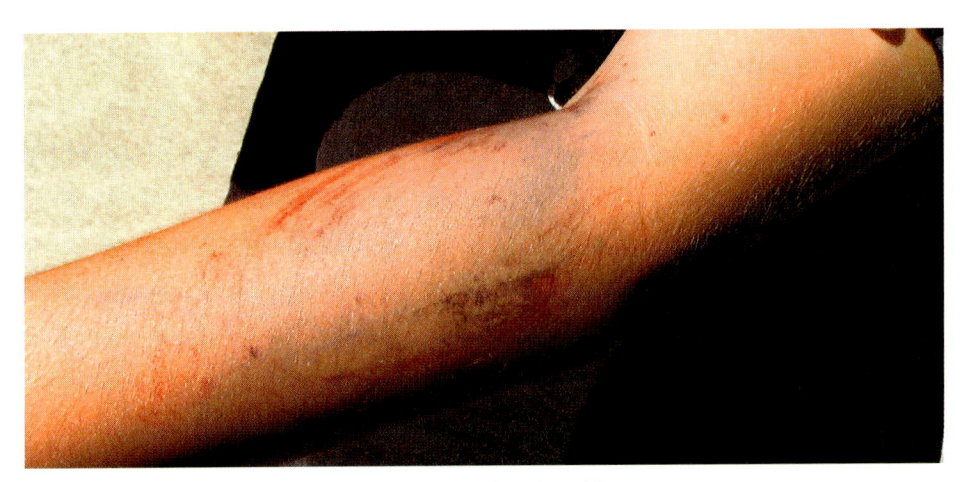

*Bruising is a result of tissue damage under the skin.*

## Steps  Internal Bleeding Treatment

1.  [BSI]
2.  [ABCH]
3.  [Step 2]
4.  [911]
5.  [Lay patient down, elevate legs]
6.  [O₂]  (See Chapter 15.)
7. Monitor the airway and remain alert for vomiting.

### Real-Life Response

The center is full of activity as the holiday season approaches. As you begin to prepare for the next project, a student aide advises you that one of the older boys cut himself. As you arrive in the room, you notice the boy is holding his hand and blood is dripping from his fingers. You also notice a small broken jar on the ground next to his desk. You see that the cut on the boy's hand is deep and bleeding profusely. Describe your treatment for this child.

# CHAPTER 13

# MUSCULOSKELETAL INJURY/IMMOBILIZATION

## LEARNING OBJECTIVES

*After completion of this chapter, the childcare provider should be able to:*

- Demonstrate how to manage a muscle or bone injury.
- Describe the general principles of splinting.
- Describe the concept of R.I.C.E. as it applies to musculoskeletal injury.

## SYMBOL INDEX

## INTRODUCTION

The human body contains over 200 bones, 600 muscles, and numerous joints. Because children are naturally curious and active, they are at increased risk for bone, muscle, or joint injury. Your chances of having to treat a musculoskeletal injury are fairly high because you care for children.

The four major types of musculoskeletal injuries are sprains, strains, dislocations, and fractures. The signs and symptoms of these musculoskeletal injuries are very similar. It is often difficult to distinguish between each type of musculoskeletal injury. A basic guideline for treating any musculoskeletal injury is to completely immobilize the injured area. "Immobilization," or splinting, is not a complicated skill nor is it difficult to learn.

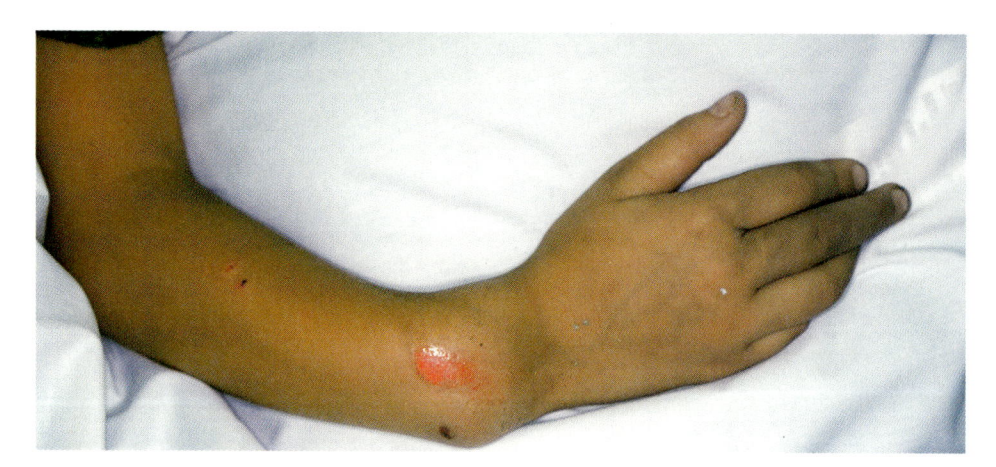

*Note the deformity in this fracture of the wrist.
(Courtesy of Charles Stewart & Associates)*

## Splinting Techniques

Splinting techniques can be applied using some very basic guidelines:

- When splinting any extremity, always attempt to immobilize the joint above and the joint below the injured area.

- Specific commercial splinting material is not necessary. Use your creativity when choosing materials for a temporary splint, for example, a pillow and cardboard. Do not worry about the look of the splint, just make sure it works!

- All splints should be lightweight, sturdy, rigid, and significantly wide and long enough to support the injured area.

- The best splint for most musculoskeletal injuries is the child's own body. For example, an injured finger can be immobilized by taping it to a finger next to it; an injured forearm can be splinted to the patient's abdomen using a sling and swathe.

*Sling and swathe.*

# Steps Musculoskeletal Injury/Immobilization

1.

2.

3. Splint the injured area and treat the injury as a fracture until proven otherwise.

4. If the injury does not involve exposed bone ends, use R.I.C.E. as explained below

**R = Rest.** This is usually accomplished by completely immobilizing the injured area. To immobilize a body part, place your splinting material next to the injured body part. Then wrap the splint with tape or gauze to keep the body part from moving. If the injured part is an arm or hand, place the part in a sling and place a pillow under the arm to support the weight. If a leg is injured, splint it to the non-injured leg to reduce movement.

**I = Ice.** Cold helps constrict blood vessels, which reduces swelling and pain. When you apply ice, make sure it is wrapped inside a plastic bag or some other material. Never place ice directly on the patient's skin.

**C = Compression.** Compression of the injured area will limit the amount of internal bleeding. To apply compression, wrap an elastic bandage around the injured area. When applying a bandage, always leave the child's fingers or toes exposed so you can monitor blood flow to these areas. If you have the bandage too tight, the fingers or toes will become cold and start turning blue. Loosen the bandage if this occurs.

**E = Elevation.** If a limb is involved, and it does not compromise the splint, elevate it above the child's heart level. This can help reduce swelling and pain.

5.

6. Activate when appropriate for the situation. Only you can determine if the injury looks serious enough to activate EMS. Consider activating EMS if the child is in significant pain or is unable to move the limb.

### Real-Life Response

You are preparing to take your three- and four-year-olds out to the playground. As they go, you see two boys pushing and shoving each other. As they exit the doors, one of the boys trips. You hear a loud cry and see one of the boys lying outside the door on the ground. As you walk up you notice the boy's left wrist is severely deformed. Describe the actions you will take in managing the child's injury.

## CHAPTER 14

# SPINAL PRECAUTIONS

### LEARNING OBJECTIVES

*After completion of this chapter, the childcare provider should be able to:*

- *Describe the importance of spinal precautions.*
- *Describe the relationship between mechanism of injury and spinal injury.*
- *Demonstrate how to properly protect a child's spinal column.*

### SYMBOL INDEX

## INTRODUCTION

One of the most potentially devastating injuries you can encounter as a childcare provider is an injury to a child's back and/or spinal cord. Serious back and spinal injuries usually affect other organ systems in the body. Any mishandling of the injury can cause fatal consequences for the child. As a childcare provider, you must be constantly aware of accidents that have an increased risk of having a "mechanism of injury" that can cause injury to the spinal cord. If a child has suffered head or neck trauma, is complaining of pain in the back, or if you suspect a fall that has occurred has the potential to cause spinal injury, IMMEDIATELY treat the child as if an actual spinal injury has occurred. Only X-rays can definitively determine if spinal injury has actually occurred.

## Treating Spinal Injuries

In cases of suspected spinal injury, open the airway using the jaw-thrust technique. This technique allows the airway to be opened without manipulation of the cervical spine. Unless absolutely necessary, all children with potential spinal injuries should be treated where they lay and manual spinal precautions should be maintained until EMS personnel arrive.

### Steps  Spinal Precautions

1. If unconscious, activate 911

2. 

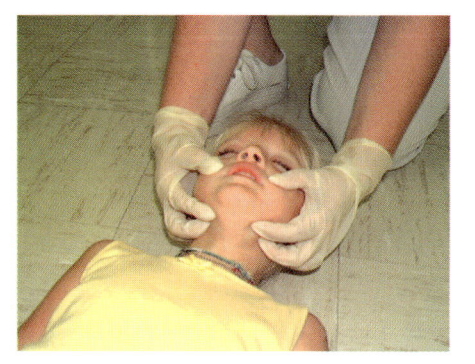

3. Open the airway using the jaw-thrust technique.

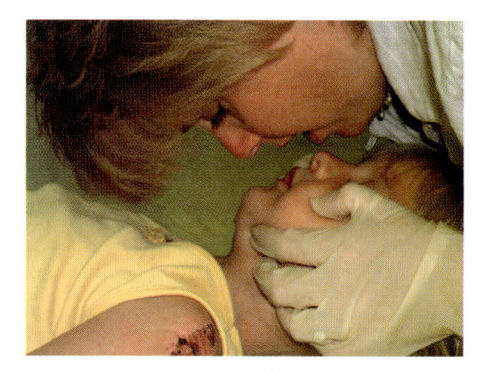

4. Assist breathing as necessary.

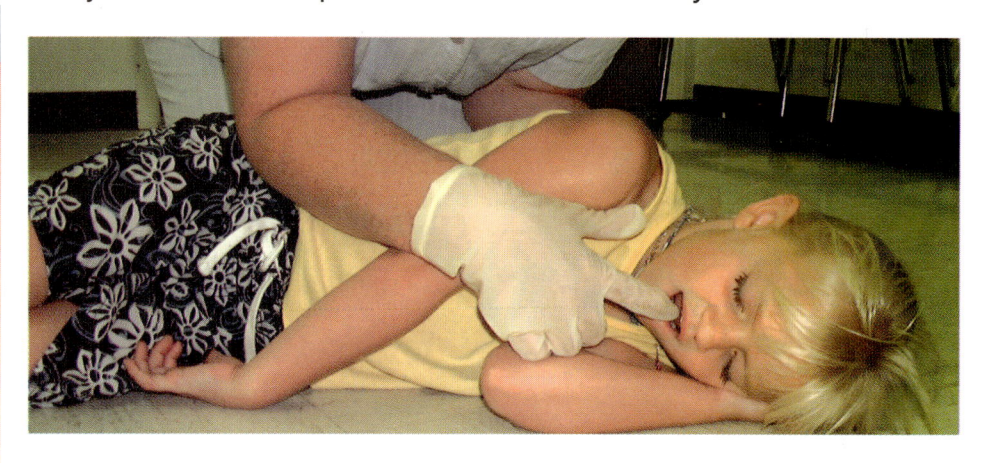

5. If the airway is not clear, roll the child as a unit, onto his or her side and clear the airway.

**DANGER!**

If you suspect possible spinal cord injury, you must immediately take spinal precautions. This includes holding the child's head still while asking questions, and using the jaw-thrust technique to open the airway.

CHAPTER 14    SPINAL PRECAUTIONS    71

6.

7. Treat any specific injuries without moving the child.

8. If absolutely necessary (i.e. fire, explosion, collapsed building) gently roll the child onto a hard flat surface, (door, cot, etc.) and move.

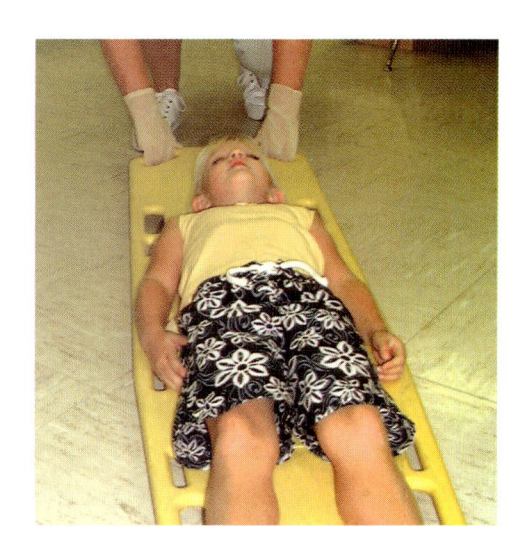

### Real-Life Response

Playing soccer with the children has been a favorite activity during the fall season. As the last game of the afternoon is coming to an end, you watch as two ten-year-old girls collide while attempting to head the ball. Both girls remain on the grass and one is rubbing her head. Samantha, however, is face down and is complaining of severe neck pain and tingling in her arms. She has a large bruise just above her left eye. Mia, the other player, is ready to get up and walk around; she says she is fine. What will you do?

# CHAPTER 15 — OXYGEN APPLICATION

## LEARNING OBJECTIVES

*After completion of this chapter, the childcare provider should be able to:*

- Describe the importance oxygen plays in normal body function.
- Describe the medical emergencies requiring oxygen application.
- Demonstrate how to properly apply medical oxygen to a child.

## SYMBOL INDEX

## INTRODUCTION

Our bodies need an adequate supply of oxygen to function correctly. We breathe in oxygen. Several illnesses (asthma, pneumonia, etc.) and injuries (fractured ribs, smoke inhalation, etc.) can adversely affect breathing and thus reduce the oxygen supply to the blood cells. As a childcare provider, you must be able to recognize when a child is not getting enough oxygen. Then you must maintain the child's airway, maintain normal breathing rates, and be sure oxygen is reaching the child's lungs.

### Signs of Oxygen Depletion

A child that is not receiving sufficient oxygen will usually complain of shortness of breath. Other signs of oxygen depletion include rapid breathing, anxiety, drowsiness, and a blue color around the

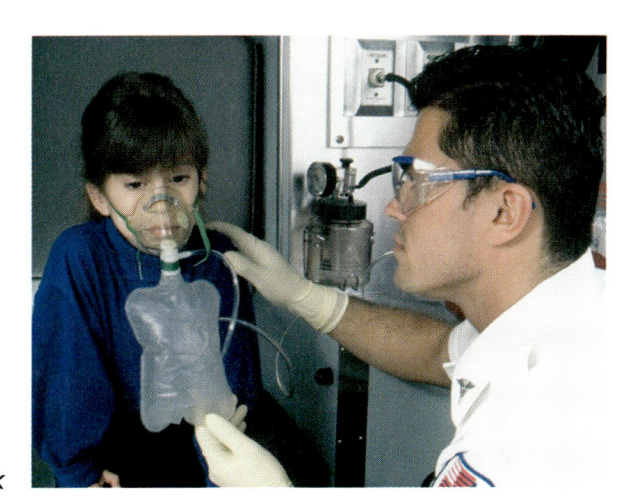

CHAPTER 15   OXYGEN APPLICATION   73

*Girl with nonbreather mask*

lips, ears, and fingernails. Many childcare facilities have an emergency medical oxygen supply.

## Oxygen Delivery Devices

You should become familiar with the operation of your specific oxygen equipment before an emergency occurs. Although medical oxygen is considered a drug, it will rarely hurt a child. If available, medical oxygen should be used whenever a child complains of shortness of breath or has any signs of breathing difficulty. Oxygen administration is also beneficial for other conditions such as asthma, bee stings, shock, abdominal pain, CPR, rescue breathing, and burns.

To deliver oxygen appropriately, you must use an appropriate oxygen delivery device. The most common device is the face mask with an oxygen reservoir attached at the bottom. Other common oxygen delivery devices designed for use with children are masks shaped like a teddy bear or a Dixie cup.

*Oxygen delivery device.*

*Teddy bear oxygen delivery device.*

## CHAPTER 15 OXYGEN APPLICATION

When determining whether to administer oxygen, a good rule of thumb is: never withhold oxygen from a child that you believe can benefit from its application.

## Steps  Oxygen Application Treatment

1.

2.

3. Determine the need for supplemental oxygen.

4. Turn on main supply valve.

5. Set liter flow to 1–15 liters per minute. In almost every emergency situation in which a child complains of shortness of breath, 12–15 liters per minute should be delivered.

6. Apply the face mask to the child.

7. Monitor the child's airway and level of consciousness.

8. Reassess the child's airway, breathing, and circulatory status.

### Real-Life Response

Hunter is a very active child who loves to explore. Other children on the playground said Hunter was chasing another boy when he stopped running and began to have difficulty breathing. The weather outside is cold and windy. Hunter has a history of asthma and states he felt an attack beginning several minutes ago. He has taken his inhaler medication without relief. What will you do?

# SECTION 3

# INJURY AND ILLNESS
## QUICK REFERENCE GUIDE

**Allergic Reaction**
**Asthma—**See *Breathing Difficulty*
**Bites (Human and Animal)**
**Bleeding, Cuts, and Scrapes**
**Breathing Difficulty**
**Bruising (Serious)**
**Burns**
**Choking**
**Cold-Related Emergencies (Hypothermia/Frostbite)**
**Croup—**See *Breathing Difficulty*
**Dental Emergencies**
**Diabetes**
**Drowning**
**Electrical Shock**
**Eye Injuries**
**Fainting and Seizures**
**Falls—Head and Neck Injuries**
**Fever**
**Fractures, Sprains, and Strains**
**Head and Neck Injuries—**See *Falls*
**Heat-Related Emergencies**
**Nosebleeds**
**Poisoning**
**Stomach Pain/Appendicitis**
**Sunburn–**See *Burns: Superficial*

# INJURY AND ILLNESS
## QUICK REFERENCE GUIDE

### INTRODUCTION

This section is designed as a quick reference guide to be used during an actual emergency. The list of injuries and illnesses is alphabetized for easy reference and represent a variety of common pediatric emergencies. The simple nature of the material capitalizes on your knowledge of each of the universal symbols covered in the previous chapters and provides only basic information necessary to treat a child before EMS arrives.

### Allergic Reaction
### (Bee and wasp stings, fire ant bites, etc.)

One of the most important steps in treating an allergic reaction is to quickly determine the child's level of respiratory distress. Although itchy eyes, hives, and runny nose are uncomfortable, an allergic reaction involving respiratory system distress is life-threatening. Signs and symptoms include:

- Hives
- Flushed face
- Blueness around mouth
- Shortness of breath
- Difficulty swallowing
- Hoarseness

Injury and Illness Quick Reference Guide 77

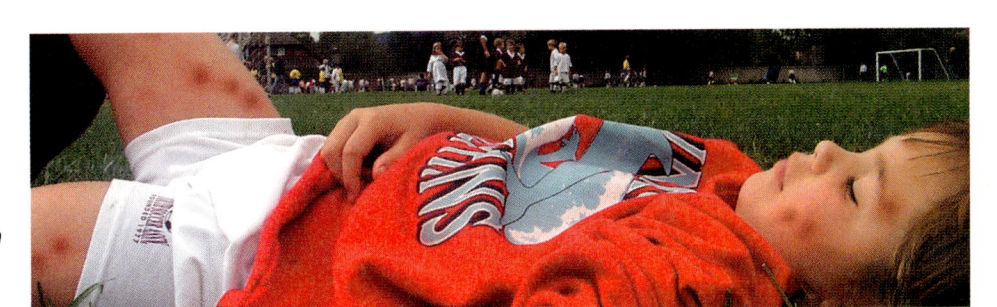

*Child with hives as a result of an allergic reaction.*

**Treatment Steps**

1. Make sure the agent that caused the reaction is not present or is not a threat to you.

2. 

3. Is the child having difficulty breathing? Are there signs of swelling of the lips, eyelids, or tongue? Is the child breaking out in hives?

4. 

5. Does the child have a known life-threatening allergy? Does the child have an Epi-pen® that is prescribed for allergic reactions? If so, assist administration of this medication now.

6. Activate the EMS system.

7. If the child stops breathing, perform rescue breathing.

8. If you lose the pulse (signs of circulation), perform CPR.

If the child has been stung by a bee or wasp, attempt to remove the stinger by scraping along the skin with a credit card or driver's license to remove it. If you cannot find anything to scrape the skin, attempt to pluck out the stinger as soon as possible. Activate the emergency notification of parents or caregivers.

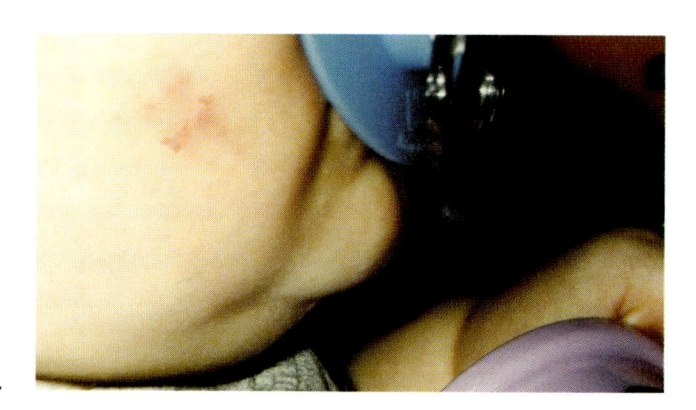

*Human bite.*

### Asthma (See *Breathing Difficulty*.)

### Bites (Human and Animal)

If the animal can be trapped in a backyard or garage, do so with caution. If the animal is still aggressive and will not let you approach the child, contact the police immediately. If a human causes the bite, be sure to properly clean the wound site as human bites have a high risk for infection.

#### Treatment Steps

1. Ensure the scene is safe.

2. Take appropriate body substance isolation precautions.

3. Perform an initial assessment.

4. If the patient is hemorrhaging, apply firm pressure directly over the wound.
    If the wound site does not involve an artery (spurting blood), cleanse the area using non-perfumed antibacterial soap and water. Apply an ice pack to the area after it is bandaged. The ice pack will reduce swelling and help with pain. Remember: never apply the ice pack directly to the skin. If the bleeding continues, apply additional bandages and direct pressure.

Injury and Illness Quick Reference Guide    79

5. If necessary, treat the child for shock.

6. If the child has any trouble breathing, give oxygen.

Initiate notification plan according to procedures and state policies. If this is an animal bite, check with your childcare licensing office regarding animal bite notification procedures. Call 911, if necessary.

## Bleeding, Cuts, and Scrapes

Minor soft-tissue wounds (small lacerations, punctures, small avulsions, abrasions)

### Treatment Steps

1. 

2. Clean wound with antibacterial soap and water.

3. Place non-adhesive bandage over the wound.

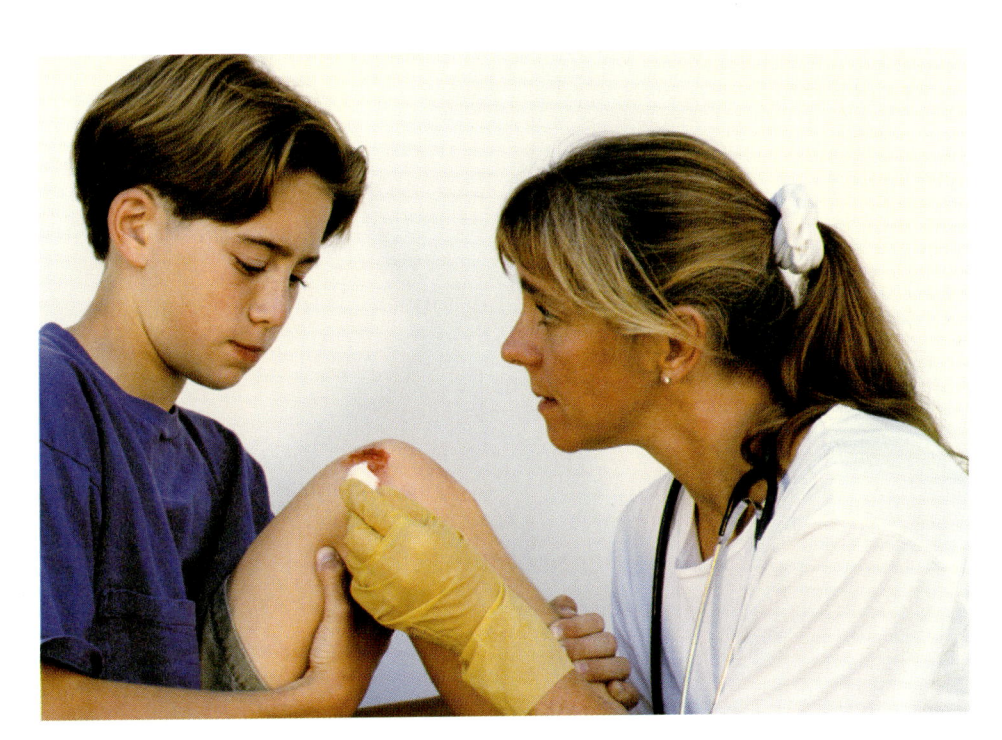

*Cleaning a child's abrasion.*

*Child using inhaler.*

## Breathing Difficulty

When a child without a medical history of a respiratory disease appears to have difficulty breathing, the child's airway may be partially or completely obstructed. This is commonly referred to as choking. The child may be gasping, wheezing, or a making high-pitched sound when they inhale. Use the appropriate treatment steps listed under the **Choking** entry. With the exception of choking, any child complaining of breathing difficulty should be treated using these steps.

### Treatment Steps

1.

2. Perform an initial assessment. Is the child coughing? If the child is coughing, encourage the child to cough and reassure him or her that you are helping. Take note of the child's color. Is the child pale? Are lips, tongue, or fingernails turning blue?

3.     4.

    If the child has prescribed medication (usually in the form of an inhaler device) for a respiratory condition such as asthma, help the child take it.

    If the child appears to be getting worse but is still coughing and you see signs of the lips or tongue turning blue, you may need to begin the steps necessary to expel an object. (See Choking.) Keep the child in an upright position, watch for any excessive drainage, and keep the airway clear.

# Injury and Illness Quick Reference Guide

## Bruising (Serious)

Ruptured blood vessels usually cause bleeding inside the tissue. The bleeding shows up as swelling and discoloration of the skin (bruising). Serious internal bleeding can be life threatening and is often not recognized until serious complications begin to take place. Signs and symptoms of serious internal bleeding include: large bruises, pain, nausea and vomiting, thirst, swelling, cold and wet skin, shortness of breath, anxiety, restlessness, decreased awareness, and bleeding from any body opening.

### Treatment Steps

1. 
2. 
3. 
4. 
5. 
6. Monitor the airway and remain alert for vomiting.

## Burns

Burns are classified as superficial, partial-thickness, and full-thickness.

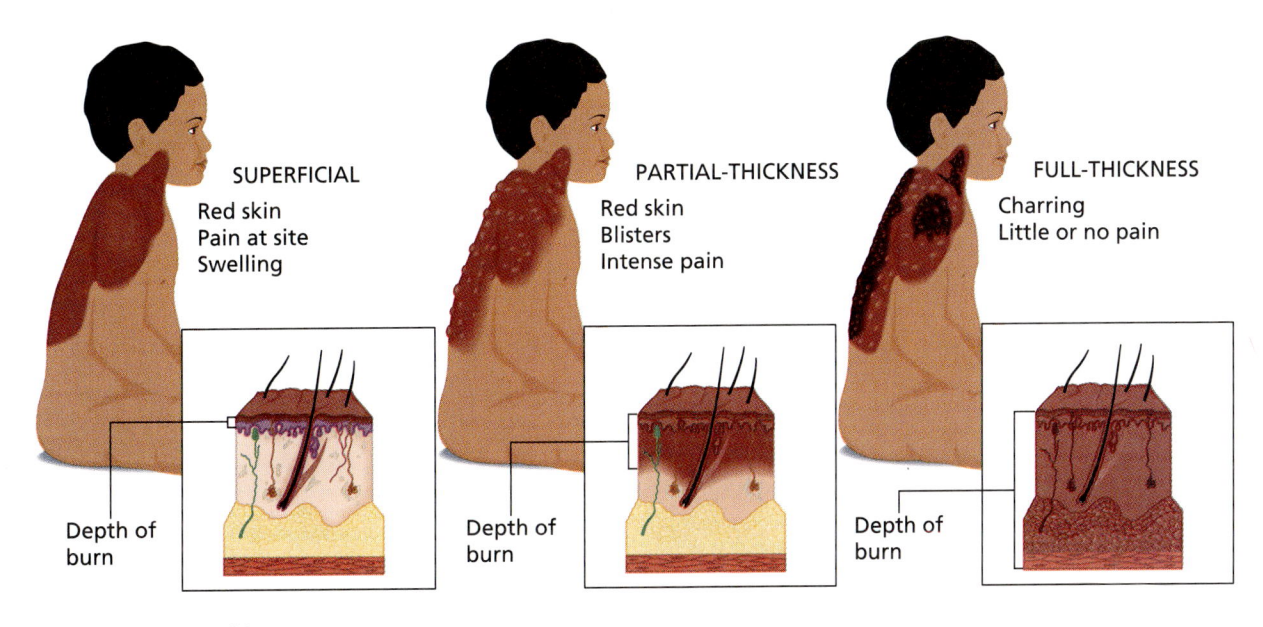

**SUPERFICIAL**
Red skin
Pain at site
Swelling

Depth of burn

**PARTIAL-THICKNESS**
Red skin
Blisters
Intense pain

Depth of burn

**FULL-THICKNESS**
Charring
Little or no pain

Depth of burn

*Three categories of burns.*

These classifications correspond to first-, second-, and third-degree burns respectively. The causes of burns are categorized into thermal (flame, steam, contact, etc.), electrical, and chemical. In all burn cases, make sure that the cause of the burn has been safely removed before you begin treatment.

### Superficial Thermal and Electrical Burns
**Treatment Steps**

1. Do not enter if you cannot ensure a safe scene.

2. Burn wounds frequently leak fluid. This fluid can be infectious.

3. Perform an initial assessment. Extinguish any fires still present: clothing, hair. Burns to the face, head, or neck could be potentially life-threatening. The airway can swell shut and cause an airway obstruction. If the burn was caused by electricity, monitor the signs of circulation frequently. Carefully remove metal belt buckles, bracelets, necklaces, earrings.

4. Activate the EMS systems.

5.    6.

If an extremity is burned, place the injured area in cool water for 20 minutes. If the injured area is not an extremity, cover the area with a cool, moist cloth. Replace the cloth with a new one every few minutes to help cool the area. Cooling reduces swelling and pain. Once the area is cooled, cover it with a dry bandage. Activate notification procedures for parents and caregivers and initiate an Incident Report.

DO NOT put any medication or remedies on the burn area.

Injury and Illness Quick Reference Guide  83

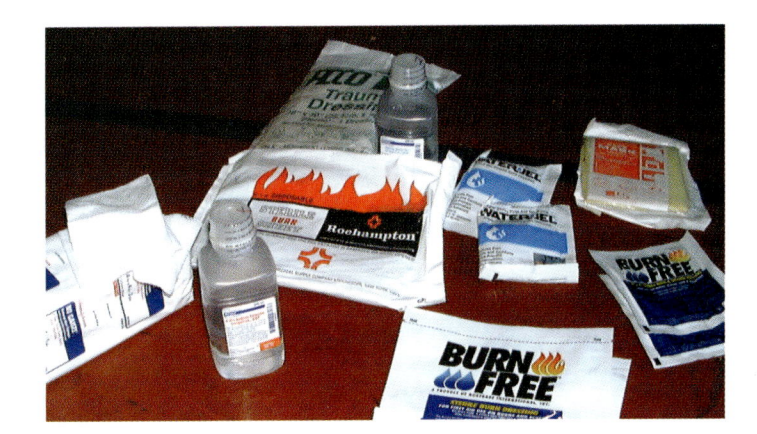

*Burn treatment items.*

### *Partial- and Full-Thickness Thermal and Electrical Burns*
**Treatment Steps**

Partial-thickness or second-degree burns cause blisters. DO NOT break the blisters. Cover the burn area with a dry bulky dressing. If burns are to face, head, neck, hands, feet, or genital area, ACTIVATE EMS IMMEDIATELY. Monitor the airway and provide life support as required.

1. Be sure the cause of the burn is no longer present.

2. Burns often bleed and release other body fluids.

3. Pay particular attention to signs of respiratory distress (change in voice, hoarseness). Observe for "soot" or discoloration in the nostrils. This could indicate inhalation of smoke or flames.

4. Activate EMS system.

5.

6. Treat for shock while waiting for EMS to arrive.

## Chemical Burns
### Treatment Steps

Chemical burns are commonly caused by a toxic dry powder or liquid chemical. For powder chemicals, the first step after ensuring personal safety is to safely brush off the powder before aggressively flushing the area with water. In some rare instances, dry powders will react violently with water. If it does, carefully brush off the powder before flushing. Test a small area first before beginning widespread flushing.

For liquid chemicals, try to quickly absorb the chemical with towels or sponges while flushing the site with water. Continue aggressive flushing until professional help arrives. If possible, try and determine the exact chemical(s) involved. Regional Poison Control Centers may offer additional information on the management of chemical burns. Check your local telephone listings for the nearest Poison Control Center or call the the National Poison Control number: 1-800-222-1222.

1. In cases involving serious toxic chemicals, wait for a Hazardous Materials team to arrive.

2. Be sure to wear protection for your eyes and mouth.

3. If possible, begin aggressive flushing with water.

4. Activate EMS system.

5.

6. Treat for shock while waiting for EMS to arrive.

# Injury and Illness Quick Reference Guide

## Choking

### Complete Airway Obstruction—Conscious Infant
**Treatment Steps**

1. Ensure the scene is safe.

2. Take appropriate body substance isolation precautions.

3. Immediately call for help. Activate the EMS system.

4. Position the infant face down on your arm or supported on your leg while sitting in a chair. Give the infant five back blows between the shoulder blades with the heel of your hand. Turn the infant over (face up). With two or three fingers, give the infant five chest thrusts in the center of their chest.

5. Reassess the airway. Look into the infant's mouth. If an object is seen, and you can reach it, remove it with your little finger. If you cannot see any object, do not put your fingers into the infant's mouth.

6. Repeat steps 4 and 5 until the object is removed, EMS arrives, or the infant loses consciousness.

7. If the infant loses consciousness before EMS arrives, initiate CPR.

### Complete Airway Obstruction—Conscious Child
**Treatment Steps**

1. Ensure that the scene is safe.

2. Take appropriate body substance isolation precautions.

3. Immediately call for help. Activate the EMS system.

4. The child will be very anxious, unable to speak or make a sound, and usually clutches his or her throat. Don't panic! Tell the child you are going to help remove the object.

5. Quickly stand behind the child or sit the child in your lap facing away from you. Hold the child tightly against your body. Place one hand in the center of the child's abdomen between the navel and where the lower ribs join the breastbone. Perform abdominal thrusts until the object is removed, the child loses consciousness, or EMS arrives.

6. If the child loses consciousness before EMS arrives, begin CPR.

## Cold-Related Emergencies (Hypothermia/Frostbite)

Cold-related injuries are a problem in many parts of the country. Talk with your local EMS representative and become familiar with the various types of cold-related emergencies common in your area. Children can suffer cold-related injuries through local cooling of a body part or total body cooling. When a person is losing body heat faster than it can be produced, the person is said to be suffering from hypothermia. This heat loss can be caused by many factors, ranging from direct or indirect contact with cool objects to wind chill. Handle any hypothermic children very gently. Even though people suffering from hypothermia do not feel pain in any area that is frozen, it is important to handle them gently to avoid causing additional injury.

*Signs and symptoms include:*

- Shivering
- Feeling of numbness
- Slow breathing
- Slow pulse
- Slurred speech
- Decreasing levels of consciousness
- Hard, cold, painless body parts

# Injury and Illness Quick Reference Guide

## Treatment Steps

1. Ensure that the scene is safe. Make sure that you are adequately protected from the elements by wearing the appropriate clothing.

2. Take appropriate body substance isolation precautions.

3. Perform an initial assessment. If possible, move the child to a warmer area.

4. If necessary, perform CPR.

5. Perform an ongoing assessment. Keep the patient still, remove all wet clothing, and cover him or her with blankets.

6. If necessary, treat the patient for shock.

7. Maintain the patient's airway. **Repeat the initial assessment as necessary**. Monitor and treat the patient's ABCH.

8. 

## Croup (See Breathing Difficulty)

## Dental Emergencies

Dental injuries, while not life threatening, usually cause a great deal of concern for the patient and childcare provider. Only a dentist can decide if a tooth can be successfully re-implanted. Careful attention must be given to keeping the tooth and socket moist.

# Injury and Illness Quick Reference Guide

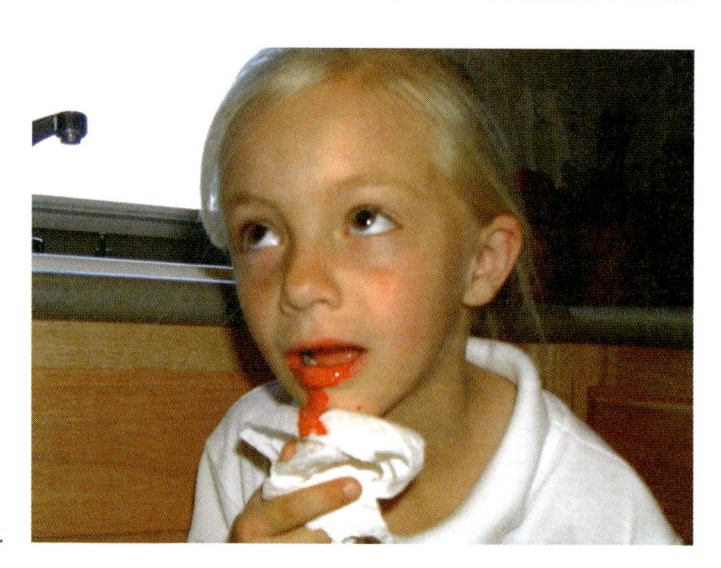

*Dental injury.*

**Treatment Steps**

1. Ensure that the scene is safe.

2. Take appropriate body substance isolation.

3. Perform an initial assessment. A child's airway takes priority over any dental injury. Be sure to limit the flow of blood into the stomach. Blood in the stomach usually causes a child to vomit. Injuries to a child's teeth usually involve some form of blunt trauma. If a tooth is broken or cracked, this could cause pain due to an exposed nerve. If the tooth is knocked out of the socket, there could be bleeding. Depending on the age of the child, place a small piece of gauze in the tooth socket to slow the bleeding. Place an ice pack on the area of the loss to slow bleeding. Dental care for children has vastly improved over the years. A "first" tooth can be re-implanted. Preserve the tooth in cold milk. DO NOT handle the tooth by the root area and DO NOT wash it off under cold water. Call parents or caregivers.

4. The child could also have a laceration of the lip. Manage this as you would other soft-tissue injuries.

## Diabetes

Diabetes is a disease that affects the body's production and use of insulin. Insulin is a hormone that controls the amount of sugar found in the bloodstream. Sugar is critical to the human body because the brain needs it in the proper amounts to function correctly. When too much or too little insulin is released into the bloodstream, the amount of sugar is altered, which in turn affects the brain's function. If this cycle is not corrected, changes in the brain's function can have tragic results. In the majority of the cases, your quick action can save the diabetic patient's life. Diabetes can begin early in childhood. This is called juvenile onset diabetes, and the patient is usually insulin-dependent.

Diabetic emergencies are usually caused by insulin shock. Insulin shock has a very sudden onset and can kill a child in a matter of minutes. The diabetic patient can experience seizures. Be prepared to protect the patient's airway.

### Treatment Steps

1. Ensure that the scene is safe.

2. Take appropriate body substance isolation precautions.

3. Perform an initial assessment.

4. Activate the EMS system.

5. Perform an ongoing assessment.

6. Administer oxygen to the patient.

7. If the child is conscious and able to swallow, have him or her eat sugar. This can be in the form of syrup, jelly, juice, honey, applesauce, or crushed sugar cubes.

8. Never give a semi-conscious patient anything by mouth. Wait for the EMS responders to arrive.

## Drowning

State regulations may not allow pools at daycare centers or the use of a pool in homes licensed for childcare. Check with your licensing agency. If a pool, irrigation ditch, or other body of water is nearby your care environment, be sure to constantly check to ensure that entrances to the area are self-locking and child safe. NEVER allow a child to play in or around water unattended. Use the buddy system (pairs of swimmers) at all times.

### Treatment Steps

1. Ensure the scene is safe.

2. Take appropriate body isolation precautions.

3. After getting the child to safety, perform an initial assessment.

4. Activate the EMS system.

5. 

6. Continue aggressive life support efforts until EMS arrives.

## Electrical Shock

Electrocution can cause a variety of serious injuries from bone fractures to cardiac arrest. A common outcome of electrocution is cardiac

# Injury and Illness Quick Reference Guide

fibrillation or standstill. Regardless of the type of injury, give careful attention to scene safety. If the source of the electricity is still exposed and live, locate the breaker box in the care center or home and cut off the electricity. If the child is still in contact with the live electrical source, attempt to remove him or her with a non-conducting object such as a wooden broom or plastic mop handle. Be careful!

## Treatment Steps

1. Ensure the scene is safe. Turn off the main power source.

2. 

3. Take appropriate body substance isolation precautions.

4. Once clear from source of the electricity, perform the initial assessment.

5. 

6. 

## Eye Injuries

### Foreign-Body Injuries

Foreign objects, such as dust, sand, eyelashes, and sawdust, cause most eye injuries. Other eye injuries can be caused by chemicals or blunt trauma (hard blow).

## Treatment Steps

1. Ensure the scene is safe.

**92** | Injury and Illness Quick Reference Guide

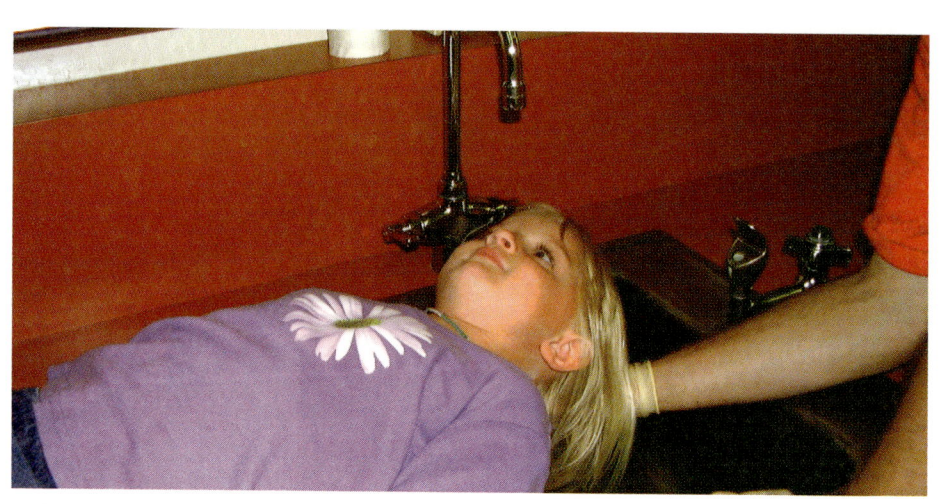

*Irrigating a child's eye.*

2. Take appropriate body isolation precautions.

3. Perform an initial assessment.

4. Irrigate the eye. Gently run water over the injured eye for at least 15 minutes. (If it is available, warm water is preferred because it causes less irritation.)

5. If the child's pain continues after the eye is irrigated, activate the EMS system and activate the notification of parents or caregivers. Cover both eyes to reduce eye movement.

If a chemical caused the eye injury, locate the chemical and call your local Poison Control Center and follow their guidelines until EMS arrives. Provide EMS with the chemical name and the information from Poison Control.

### *Blunt Trauma and Eye Lacerations*
**Treatment Steps**

1.    2.    3.

# Injury and Illness Quick Reference Guide

4. If the child suffered a blunt trauma eye injury, take spinal precautions.

5. If an area around the eye is bleeding, apply light pressure to control the bleeding. If there is an impaled object in the eye, do not attempt to remove it. Stabilize the object by placing a bulky dressing around the object to secure it in place. This may be very difficult with a child. Another provider is essential for this procedure with a child. If you are alone, hold the object with your gloved hand and wait for EMS. If the child has suffered blunt trauma around the eye, place an ice pack over the area. This helps reduce swelling.

   If the child has a lacerated eye, immediately cover the eye. Covering both eyes is the preferred method, but this may be very difficult with a child. If the child will not tolerate this, just cover the injured eye. Also keep the child in a room with minimal lighting and no other children around until EMS arrives.

6.

## Fainting and Seizures

### Fainting

Fainting can be caused by a number of problems. A child may become exhausted from too much physical activity and faint. Nutritional problems and underlying medical problems can also cause fainting. ALWAYS make sure the airway is open and the child is breathing.

### Treatment Steps

1.

2.

**94** ■■■ Injury and Illness Quick Reference Guide

3. Fainting spells should last no longer than 1–2 minutes. If they last longer, activate EMS.

4. If the child awakens before EMS arrives, place the child in a position of comfort, keep him or her quiet, and activate parent or caregiver notification. Record all the events of the incident.

5. Carefully monitor the child's airway.

### Seizures

Like fainting, seizures are the result of a variety of problems. Regardless of the cause, seizures can be life-threatening if allowed to continue for long periods of time. A majority of seizures are self-limiting and stop within a few minutes. Efforts must be made to keep seizing children from injuring themselves.

### Treatment Steps

1.

2.

3. Clear the area of any hazards that could injure the child. Determine if the child has a history of seizures. If there is a history of past seizure activity, is this seizure any different than the last one or the parents' history? Record the length of the seizure activity and the child's action during the seizure. Remove other children from the area.

4. Do not wait. Activate immediately.

After the seizure has stopped, place a pillow under the child's head. Protect the airway and wait for EMS to arrive if you called them. Activate your notification procedures for the child's parent or caregiver. A child will be exhausted after a seizure. Keep the child in a quiet area and do not leave the child alone.

## Falls—Head and Neck Injuries

All children with significant face or head injuries should be treated as if they have an accompanying spinal injury. Many children with head injuries become sick and vomit. Be alert for vomiting and always maintain a clear and open airway. Some head-injured children will at first appear fine and then rapidly lose consciousness.

Children with severe facial injuries usually have airway problems. If you notice the child has a puncture wound in the throat and you hear a sucking sound, quickly cover the wound with your gloved hand.

Hundreds of tiny blood vessels along with several larger arteries cover the head and face. Consequently, even a small cut on the head or face can bleed excessively. Even though a wound may be minor, the excessive bleeding can add anxiety to the situation.

Head injuries are commonly classified into two categories: <u>open</u> and <u>closed</u> head injuries. Open injuries expose brain tissue and closed injuries involve an intact skull. Both types of head injury can include similar signs and symptoms including:

- Confusion, combativeness, unconsciousness
- Bruises, lacerations, and avulsions
- Deformity of the skull
- Bruising around the eyes and behind the ears
- Fluid leaking from the ears and/or nose
- Pain or tenderness to the scalp
- Nausea and/or vomiting
- Paralysis or disability
- Seizures

## Treatment Steps

Injuries involving the head and neck require careful consideration for both the child's airway and spinal column. Any unnecessary movement can have grave consequences! ALWAYS assume that a child suffering a serious head injury has simultaneously injured the spinal cord. Maintain an open airway using the jaw-thrust method and keep the child still until EMS arrives.

1.

2. Pay particular attention to the airway; make sure it remains clear of blood, vomit, etc.

3.   4.

5.   6.   7.

## FEVER

The safest method for obtaining a temperature from an infant is by using a tympanic electronic thermometer. Follow the direction for use. Record the temperature. If the temperature is between 100°–102° F, administer fever medication, ONLY IF PRESCRIBED BY A HEALTH CARE PROFESSIONAL AND PRIOR PERMISSION IS GIVEN. Only administer the prescribed dosage indicated on the container.

### Treatment Steps

1.

2. Perform an initial assessment. Evaluate the child for dehydration. How often have diapers been changed? Has there been any vomiting? Examine the fontanelle (soft spot on top of the infant's head —birth to 6 months). Is it sunken? This child may be dehydrated due to an illness or infection. Initiate parent notification if this level of temperature is in your exclusionary policy.

3. An infant or young child with a temperature of 100°–102° F should be closely observed. High temperatures can cause febrile seizures. Cooling the child with a tepid (slightly cool and moist) cloth is essential at this time. If seizure activity develops, activate EMS.

# Injury and Illness Quick Reference Guide

4. Maintain open airway and continue to cool the infant until EMS arrives.

## FRACTURES, SPRAINS, AND STRAINS

Musculoskeletal injuries, while painful, are rarely life-threatening. Fractures and dislocations can cause deformity to the area. However, do not spend time trying to determine if the child has suffered a sprain or a fracture or dislocation. Focus on keeping the injured area still and free from movement. Splint the injured area and the joints above and below the injury site. The child's own body is often the best available splinting material. Musculoskeletal injuries involving a joint can disrupt the normal development of bone or muscle. Therefore, further treatment should be given by a local orthopedic specialist. General treatment for musculoskeletal injuries includes R.I.C.E. (See Chapter 13.)

### Treatment Steps

1. Ensure that the scene is safe.

2. Take appropriate body substance isolation precautions.

3. Perform an initial assessment.

4. Perform an ongoing assessment. Determine whether the muscle or bone injury is an open or closed fracture.

5. If the child complains of pain and your assessment reveals swelling or discoloration of the area, treat the site as if it was broken. Use the R.I.C.E. treatment method.

6. Treat for shock.

7. If necessary, activate the EMS system. Activate notification of parent or caregiver.

## HEAD AND NECK INJURIES (See *Falls*.)

## HEAT-RELATED EMERGENCIES

Prolonged exposure to excessive heat can cause the body to malfunction. The body will generally compensate for the exposure through sweating and increased breathing. Eventually, the body is unable to cool itself fast enough and heat begins to build up internally. As the temperature rises, heat-related complications ranging from heat cramps to heat stroke appear.

Heat cramps involve cramping of the large muscles (usually abdominal and leg muscles). Heat exhaustion involves excessive sweating, pale ashen skin, and a changing level of consciousness. Heat stroke, which is evidenced by very red and hot skin and no obvious sweating, is a life-threatening condition and requires immediate and aggressive treatment.

It can be difficult to differentiate between these heat-related conditions. If you are unable to determine the exact heat-related condition, treat for heat stroke until EMS arrives.

### Heat Cramps and Heat Exhaustion
**Treatment Steps**

1.

2.

3. Remove the child to a cool area. Help cool the child by applying damp towels or other materials to his or her skin. If the child is fully conscious, have him or her drink cool water or cool fruit juice every 20 minutes until symptoms improve.

4. If child does not improve, perform ongoing assessment.

# Injury and Illness Quick Reference Guide

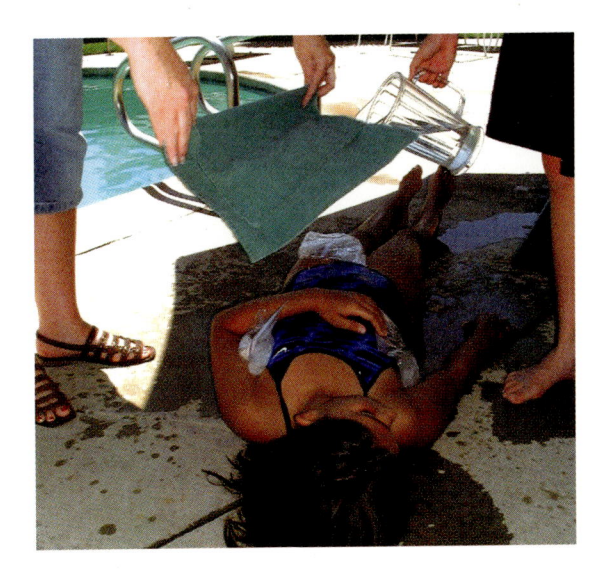

*Rapidly cooling child that has heat stroke.*

5. 🆘 Activate the EMS system. Initiate parent or caregiver notification.

## Heat Stroke
### Treatment Steps

1. 🔥 Remove child to a cool location while providing care.

2. ☣️

3. 🆘    4. 🆘

5. Rapidly cool the child. This is a life-threatening emergency. Place damp cloths and ice packs on the groin and armpits. Fan the patient aggressively. Await EMS.

## NOSEBLEEDS

A nosebleed is a common childhood injury usually caused by either blunt force or spontaneous rupture of small blood vessels. In any case involving blunt force, give special consideration to the possibility of associated neck injury and injuries to the cheeks, eye sockets, and jaw. Limit movement until EMS arrives.

**Injury and Illness Quick Reference Guide**

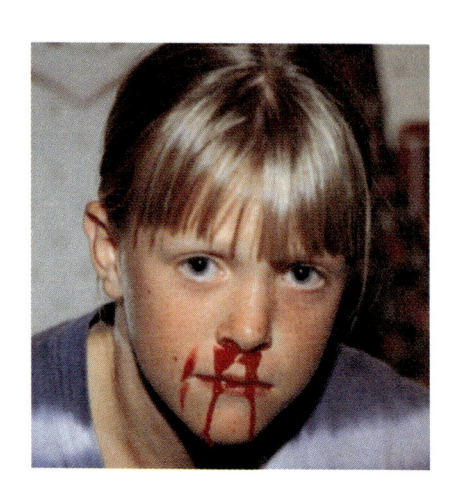

*Child with nosebleed.*

In all nosebleed situations, try to limit the amount of blood draining into the back of the child's airway by keeping the child sitting up with head down. Excessive blood in the stomach can cause nausea and vomiting.

### Treatment Steps

1. Ensure the scene is safe.

2. Take appropriate body substance isolation procedures.

3. Perform an initial assessment. If the nose does not look deformed, pinch the child's nostrils together. Then apply an ice pack at the bridge of the nose.

4. If blunt force (punch, striking an object, etc.) was involved, stabilize head and neck.

5. If bleeding persists, initiate notification procedures according to policies. If necessary, activate the EMS system.

## POISONING

Chemicals and other toxic substances are found in almost every occupational setting and every home. Occasionally, these substances poison children. Poisons can enter the body four ways: ingestion, inhalation, absorption (through the skin), or injection. They can also enter the body in any combination of these ways. When treating a child of poisoning, pay particular attention to the initial assessment. The child's ABCH can deteriorate rapidly.

After you do the initial assessment, attempt to gather as much information about the substance as quickly as possible. If possible, ask the child or any bystanders what was ingested, when it was ingested, and approximately how much was ingested. Be prepared to relate this information to the responding EMS team. If time allows, attempt to locate the poison to give to the EMS team. You may also want to contact your local Poison Control Center for additional information about how to treat your patient. These centers specialize in poisonings and overdoses. Most EMS professionals will call them as soon as they arrive on scene. Find out the phone number of your closest Poison Control Center and post it near every phone or use the National Poison Control number: 1-800-222-1222.

### Treatment Steps

1. Ensure the scene is safe.

2. Take appropriate body substance isolation procedures.

3. Activate the EMS system.

4. Perform an initial assessment.

5. If necessary, deliver artificial ventilations to the patient.

# Injury and Illness Quick Reference Guide

6. If necessary, perform CPR.

7. Administer oxygen to the patient.

8. Perform an ongoing assessment.

## Stomach Pain/Appendicitis

The abdominal region contains several vital organs. They include the liver, stomach, colon, pancreas, spleen, and kidneys. Abdominal emergencies are a challenge to even the most experienced childcare provider. These types of emergencies are often difficult to assess and manage. Children suffering from abdominal emergencies will complain of generalized pain and discomfort. They are often unable to pinpoint the exact location of their pain. Abdominal emergencies can be caused by blunt trauma, such as a direct blow; penetrating trauma, such as a stabbing; diseases, such as cancer; blockages, such as an impacted bowel.

### Treatment Steps

1. Ensure the scene is safe.

2. Take appropriate body substance isolation procedures.

3. Perform an initial assessment. Be sure to control any external bleeding that you find.

4. Perform an ongoing assessment.

# Injury and Illness Quick Reference Guide

5. Activate the EMS system.

6. Administer oxygen to the patient. *If available, in every case.*

7. If necessary, treat the patient for shock.

8. When treating a patient with exposed abdominal organs, never attempt to place the organs back in the abdominal cavity. Rather, cover them with a clean, moist cloth. Then treat the patient for shock, administer oxygen, monitor the patient's ABCH, and activate the EMS system.

## Sunburn (See *Burns: Superficial*)

# ANSWERS TO REAL-LIFE RESPONSE TREATMENT QUESTIONS

### Chapter 4
Obviously live power lines present a serious danger to all on scene. These wires are unpredictable and can jump around violently as they strike the ground. In this situation, advise the children to move as far away from the power line as possible. Contact EMS immediately. Do not attempt to control the power line. If the small boy who fell is injured and is at risk from being hit by the power line, have the older children carefully drag the child away from the dangerous area.

### Chapter 5
Ensure that the scene is safe, then take standard precautions by donning gloves. Do not attempt to stop the bleeding without the appropriate personal protective equipment. Given the nature of the injury, you should determine if the child is complaining of head or neck pain. If so, take spinal precautions and do not allow the child to move his head or neck until EMS arrives.

### Chapter 6
Assuming scene safety and standard precautions have been considered, Susan's first treatment should be to complete an initial assessment and correct any life-threatening conditions found. Since Susan seems flustered, you may suggest that you take over and help. EMS should be activated as soon as possible.

### Chapter 7
Once scene safety, standard precautions, and the initial assessment are completed, complete the ongoing assessment. This assessment will not only help identify the injuries the child is complaining of, but injuries that the child may not realize he has. Given the mechanism of injury, efforts should be made to stabilize the child's head and neck by using spinal precautions.

## Chapter 8

First, when traveling away from the day-care facility with a group of children, you should consider the possibility that an injury might occur and take a portable or cell phone. Second, ensure that you know the medical history of each child in your care, especially identifying children with allergies.

## Chapter 9

The child appears to be suffering a complete airway obstruction. This is a life-threatening condition that requires immediate action. Begin the techniques for a complete foreign-body airway obstruction in a child. This includes wrapping your arms around the child and performing abdominal thrusts (Heimlich maneuver) until the object dislodges or the child loses consciousness. Have someone activate EMS immediately. If necessary, initiate basic life support/cardiopulmonary resuscitation.

## Chapter 10

When an unresponsive child shows signs of circulatory problems, you should take standard precautions and then immediately complete the initial assessment. Depending on the outcome of the assessment, you may need to perform rescue breathing/artificial ventilation and basic life support/cardiopulmonary resuscitation. Activate the EMS system as soon as possible.

## Chapter 11

This child is showing serious signs of hypovolemic shock and needs immediate assistance from EMS. Use standard precautions and conduct the initial assessment. Next, activate EMS immediately and initiate treatment for hypovolemic shock. Give attention to ABCH.

## Chapter 12

Although the bleeding appears serious, you must take standard precautions before initiating emergency care. Complete the initial assessment, paying particular attention to the "H" of the initial assessment—controlling bleeding. Then complete the ongoing assessment and consider treatment for hypovolemic shock. If bleeding cannot be controlled, activate EMS as soon as possible.

## Chapter 13

After performing an initial assessment, initiate R.I.C.E. and make the appropriate notification.

## Chapter 14

Cervical spine injuries are very serious and special attention must be given to any situation that include injuries to the head or neck. Both players have the potential for spinal injuries, and spinal precautions must be taken. Complete the initial assessment of both players using standard precautions. Correct all life-threatening conditions and complete the ongoing assessment on both players to rule out the possibility of additional injuries. Activate EMS as soon as possible. Treat the soft-tissue injuries as time allows.

## Chapter 15

Hunter needs immediate help. Immediately activate EMS and take standard precautions. Complete an initial assessment to determine the status of Hunter's breathing. Consider rescue breathing/artificial ventilation if Hunter's breathing is inadequate. If available, begin oxygen administration immediately. Complete an ongoing assessment to rule out other causes of Hunter's shortness of breath.

## A

ABCH assessment process, 33–34, 37, 103
    airway, 33
    breathing, 33
    circulation, 34
    hemorrhage, 34
Abdominal emergencies, 102
Abdominal pain, 73
Abdominal thrusts, 47
Abrasions, 60, 79
Age-appropriate safety guidelines
    for infants, 6
    for older children, 7
    for toddlers and preschoolers, 7
AIDS, 29
Airway
    bleeding into, 59
    clearing, 33, 43, 70
Airway obstruction
    complete, 45–46, 47
      in children, 85–86
      in infant, 85
    foreign body in, 45–46
    partial, 45, 47
      in children, 47
      in infants, 45
Allergic reaction, 76–77
American Heart Association, 35, 51, 53
American Red Cross, 21
Amputation, 60, 63
Anaphylactic shock, 56
Animal bites, 78–79
Appendicitis, 102–103
Artificial ventilation, 42–48, 49
Assessment
    initial, 32–35, 42–43
    ongoing, 36–39
Asthma, 73, 80
Avulsions, 60, 62, 79

## B

Back injuries, 39
Basic life support
    cardiopulmonary resuscitation, 49–54
    rescue breathing, 42–48
Bathroom, PediScan checklist for, 13–19
Bee stings, 73, 76–77
Biohazard containers, 31
Bites, 78–79
Black eye, 63
Bleeding, 59, 79
    into airway, 59
    external, 59, 61–63
    internal, 63–64, 81
    nose, 99–100

Bloodborne pathogens, cardiopulmonary resuscitation and, 50
Blunt trauma, 102
Body substance isolation, 29. *See also* Standard precautions
Brachial artery, 62
Breathing
    assessing, 33
    difficulties in, 80
    rescue, 34, 42–48, 73
Bruising, 63, 81
Buddy system, 90
Burns, 73, 81–84. *See also* Fire
    chemical, 84
    electrical, 82–83
    full-thickness, 81
    partial-thickness, 81, 83
    superficial, 81
    thermal, 82–83

## C

Cardiac arrest, 42, 90
Cardiac fibrillation, 91
Cardiopulmonary resuscitation, 49–54, 73
    bloodborne pathogens and, 50
    common problems during, 54
    two-person techniques, 54
Centers for Disease Control (CDC), 29
Chain of survival, 50
Chemical burns, 84
Chest compressions, 34
    in children, 51–53
    in infants, 53
Chest thrusts, 46
Children
    age-appropriate safety guidelines for, 7
    chest compressions in, 51–53
    complete airway obstruction in, 47, 85–86
    medical information for, 8
    medication administration to, 8–9
    partial airway obstruction in, 47
    rescue breathing in, 44–45
    underestimating, 4
Choking, 80, 85–86
Circulation, assessing, 34
Closed head injuries, 95
Cold-related emergencies, 86–87
Communicable disease, 29
Complete airway obstruction, 45–46, 47
    in children, 85–86
    in infant, 85
Compression ventilation ratio, 54
Contusion, 60
Croup. *See* Breathing, difficulties in
Cuts, 79

# Index

**D**

Dental emergencies, 87–88
Diabetes, 89–90
Disaster planning, 20–24
    available resources, 24
    determining preparedness, 20–21
    developing plan, 21–22
    emergency disaster kit, 22–23
    natural disasters in, 23–24
    safe room/evacuation plan, 22
Dislocations, 65, 97–98
Disposable gloves, 30
Drowning, 90

**E**

Earthquakes, 24
Electrical burns, 82–83
Electrical shock, 90–91
Emergency disaster kit, 22–23
Emergency medical services, x, 27
    activation of, 3, 27, 33, 40–41, 50, 83
    response times by, 3
Epi-pen®, 77
Evaluation plan, 22
External bleeding, 59, 61–63
Eye injuries, 91–93

**F**

Face masks, 73
Fainting, 93–94
Falls, 95–96
Federal Emergency Management Agency (FEMA), 21
Femoral artery, 62
Fever, 96–97
Fire. *See also* Burns
    basic facts, 9–12
Fire ant bites, 75
Fire drills, 11
First aid kits
    contents of basic, 18–19
    special, 19
Floods, 23
Foreign bodies
    in airway obstruction, 45–46
    in injuries, 91–93
Fractures, 65, 97–98
Frostbite, 86–87

**G**

Good Samaritan laws, x

**H**

Hallway, PediScan checklist for, 15
Handwashing, 30
Head injuries, 39, 95–96
Head-tilt chin-lift, 33, 43, 44
Heat cramps, 98
Heat exhaustion, 98
Heat stroke, 98, 99
Hemorrhaging, 61, 78
    checking for, 34
Hepatitis B, 29
Human bites, 78–79
Hurricanes, 23–24
Hypothermia, 86–87
Hypovolemic shock, 55

**I**

Ice packs, 78
Immobilization, 65–68
    spinal precautions, 69–71
Incident Report Form, 3–4, 5
Infants
    age-appropriate safety guidelines for, 6
    chest compressions in, 53
    complete airway obstruction in, 45–46, 85
    partial airway obstruction in, 45
    rescue breathing in, 43–45
Infectious disease, 29
Initial assessment, 32–35, 42–43
Injury prevention, xii, 2–3
    emergency medical services response times and, 3
    strategies in, 4, 6
Injury reporting, 3–4, 5
Impaled objects, 93
Insect/Bee Sting Kit, 19
Insect stings, 56, 73, 76–77
Insulin, 89
Insulin shock, 89
Internal bleeding, 63–64, 81

**J**

Jaw-thrust maneuver, 33, 70, 95

**K**

Kitchen, PediScan checklist for, 15–16

**L**

Lacerations, 59, 60, 79
    eye, 93
Legal protection, x

**M**

Mechanism of injury, 27, 69
Medical alert medallions, 36
Medical information, 8
Medication administration, 8–9
Musculoskeletal injuries, 65–68, 97–98
    R.I.C.E. for, 67–68, 97
    splinting, 66

# Index

## N
Natural disasters, 23–24
Nature of illness, 27
Neck injuries, 33, 34, 95–96
Nosebleeds, 99–100

## O
Ongoing assessment, 36–39
Open head injuries, 95
Oxygen delivery devices, 73–74
Oxygen depletion, signs of, 72–73

## P
Partial airway obstruction, 45, 47
    in children, 47
    in infants, 45
PediScan checklist, 13–19
    for bathroom, 14
    for general indoor areas, 17
    for general safety guidelines, 17
    for hallway, 15
    for kitchen, 15–16
    for play areas/playground, 16
    for sleeping area, 16–17
Penetrating trauma, 102
Personal protective devices, 30–31, 44
Play areas/playground, PediScan checklist for, 16
Poison Control Center, 84, 92, 101
Poison First-Aid Kit, 19
Poisoning, 101–102
Preschoolers, age-appropriate safety guidelines for, 7
Pressure points, 34, 62
Punctures, 60, 79

## R
Rescue breathing, 34, 42–48, 73
    in children, 44–45
    in infants, 43–45
Respiratory arrest, 42
Respiratory distress, signs of, 83
Responsiveness, checking for, 33, 51
R.I.C.E. for musculoskeletal injuries, 67–68, 97

## S
Safe room, 22
Safety, teaching, 4
Scene safety, 26–28
    evaluation of, 28
    mechanism of injury, 27
    nature of illness, 27
Scrapes, 79
Seizures, 89, 94
Septic shock, 55–56

Shock, 55–57, 73
    anaphylactic shock, 56
    electrical, 90–91
    hypovolemic, 55
    septic, 55–56
    treatment for, 56
Sleeping area, PediScan checklist for, 16–17
Smoke alarms, 11
Snakebite Kit, 19
Soft-tissue injuries, 58–64, 79
    treatment for, 60–64
    types of, 59–60
Spinal injuries
    precautions with, 69–71
    treating, 70–71
Splinting, 61, 65
    techniques in, 66
Sprains, 65, 97–98
Standard precautions, 29–31, 50
    bloodborne pathogens and, 50
    personal protective devices, 30–31, 44
Stomach pain, 102–103
Strains, 65, 97–98
Sunburn. *See* Burns

## T
Thermal burns, 82–83
Toddlers, age-appropriate safety guidelines for, 7
Tornadoes, 24
Tuberculosis, 29

## U
Universal precautions, 29
Universal symbols, ix, xi, 25

## X
Xiphoid process, 47, 52
X-rays, 69